Classic

NEW ENGLAND STORIES

Classic
NEW ENGLAND STORIES

True Tales and Tall Tales of Character and Culture

EDITED *by*
JAKE ELWELL

THE LYONS PRESS

GUILFORD, CONNECTICUT

AN IMPRINT OF THE GLOBE PEQUOT PRESS

In memory of Gram
Esther E. Elwell
Who made a home for us in New England

The Lyons Press is an imprint of The Globe Pequot Press.

10   9   8   7   6   5   4   3   2   1

Printed in the United States of America

Book design by Claire Zoghb

ISBN 1-59228-213-X

Library of Congress Cataloging-in-Publication Data
is available on file.

Contents

CONTENTS

Acknowledgments

Thanks to Tony Lyons and Thomas Meagher at The Lyons Press for shepherding and hand-holding, and to Shira Handler and Karyn Marcus for photocopying. Thanks to English teachers Mike Wentworth, Harvard Knowles, and Robert Greenfield. And, of course, thanks and love always to Lisa and the boys.

Introduction

I submit that it should not be much of a stretch for most readers to accept the concept of New England as a microcosm of the world.

Consider the bounty found in those six states, the sheer variety—of person, of scenery, of education, of history and experience. Just think! The intrepid traveler can start his day with blueberry pancakes among the lobster pots in coastal Maine, ski the morning away in Vermont, and depart in time for high tea in Boston. Following a large Italian dinner in Providence, he can bed down in New Haven, Connecticut (stopping along the way to see his insurance broker in Hartford), all without setting foot outside of New England.

It is hoped that some of the spectrum of the New England experience is replicated in the arrangement of these stories. They proceed roughly from "dark" to "light." From the dark of doom and death of

Melville's New Bedford to the light of carelessness, pluck, and youth in the "brite" laughingstockyards of Henry Shute's New Hampshire. Amongst this gathering of tales tall, literate, droll, and tragic, are the hallmarks of the Yankee *welt* as it has been understood.

Firstly, the physical place of New England, in all its variety, from deep urban to far rural. Compare Hale's Christmas in Boston with Jewett's Maine coast; contrast Hawthorne's devotion to the hearth of home with the wanderlust suffusing Melville's cobblestoned streets.

And New England's people. From peripatetic port-city dwellers like Aldrich's Rivermouth denizens, to Sarah Orne Jewett's housebound Marsh Rosemary—and all in between—all are equally "Yankee."

The language, by turns laconic, cutting, archaic, and almost always "local." Many New England stories written before the twentieth century are, in fact, almost illegible to the reader in the twenty-first, laden as they are with localisms, wrong turns of phrase, and undecodable contractions. Of this, Jewett's "Law Lane" provides a taste.

And, of course, unavoidably, there is history throughout these stories, as there is throughout New England. It's a region that (justifiably) embraces its history, depending on it for identity, status, and, not least, for money. At the same time, one needs only to look at Melville's Nantucket to see that New England is hardly stuck in time. In fact, the New England we "know" is largely a creation of the industrial revolution, a reinvented, mostly rural, wonderworld created as compensation for, or escape from, the grimy factories and slums that sprang up across New England. It's no accident that many of these stories date from that era.

Still and all, history and tradition reign and cannot be avoided in New England (where even rebellion and dissent are traditional). The final two stories in this collection, of Thanksgiving and Christmas, celebrate New England's intimate tie to tradition and provide an ending (perhaps unlikely, given New England's notorious weather) decidedly "light."

Old Deb and Other Old Colony Witches

[WILLIAM ROOT BLISS]

"After you pass Carver Green on the old road from the bay to Plymouth," said one of these women, "you will see a green hollow in a field. It is Witches' Hollow, and is green in winter and summer, and on moonlit nights witches have been seen dancing in it to the music of a fiddle played by an old black man. I never saw them, but I know people who saw witches dancing there. In a small house near the hollow, a little old woman lived who was a witch; she went by the name of Old Betty, and she danced on the green with the devil as a partner. There was an old man who lived in that neighborhood by himself; he was kind to Betty, giving her food and firewood. After a while he got tired of her and told her she must keep away. One day he caught her there and put her in a bag, and locked the bag in a closet, and put the key in his pocket, and went away to his work. While he was gone, she got out of the bag and unlocked the door. Then she got his pig, dog, cat, and rooster, put them into the bag, put the bag in the closet and hid herself. When the man came home the animals in the bag were making a dreadful noise. 'Ah, ha! Old Betty, there you are!' said the man. He took the bag and dashed it on his doorstone, and the old woman laughed and cried out, 'You hain't killed Old Betty yet!'"

Another story told by the old women was of two witches who lived in Plymouth woods, near the head of Buzzard's Bay, who never went out in the daytime; but in the evening twilight they walked out "casting spells." They cast a spell on a boy, compelling him to follow them home. Putting him to bed in a lower room, they went up a ladder into the loft. At midnight the boy saw them come down the ladder, go to the oven, and take out a quahog shell. Each witch rubbed it behind her ears and said "Whisk!" when each flew up the chimney. The boy got up and rubbed the shell behind his ears; immediately he went up the chimney and found himself standing outdoors beside the witches, who were sitting astride black horses in the yard. On seeing the boy one of them dismounted, went into the house and returned with a "witch bridle" and a bundle of straw. She flung the bridle over the straw, and out of it came a pony. The boy was put on the pony's back, and away the three cantered across a large meadow, until they came to a brook. The witches cleared the brook at a leap; but the boy, when he cleared it, said to his pony, "A pretty good jump for a lousy calf!" Those words broke the spell; the pony vanished, the boy stood alone with the bridle and the straw. He now ran after the witches, and soon he came to an old deserted house in which he heard the sound of fiddles. He peeped in a window and saw a black man fiddling, and the two witches and other old women dancing around him. Frightened, he ran down the road until he came to a farmhouse. He knocked on the door, was admitted, and the next day the farmer carried him to his parents.

The old women who told the witch stories said that their grandmother had been personally acquainted with two witches, in the last century. One of these was named Deborah Borden, called at that day "Deb Burden," who was supposed to have caused a great deal of mischief in Wareham, Rochester, and Middleboro. It was thought to be necessary for farmers to keep in her good graces lest she should cause a murrain to come upon cattle, lest the rye refuse to head, and the corn to ear. She was a weaver of cloth and rag carpets. Woe to the unlucky housewife who worried Deb or hurried her at her looms! I will let one of the sisters relate her story of this sorceress. It is not probable that the relator had ever heard of Robert Burns' story of Tam

O'Shanter and his gray mare Meg; but a running brook filled the same place in that story and in this:—

"Once my grandmother had a web of cloth in Deb's looms, so she sent my mother and a girl named Phebe after it. The two girls were just as intimate as finger and thumb. They went to Deb's house and told her what my grandmother said, and it made her mad, 'cause she didn't like to be hurried. Near her back door was a tree full of red apples, and Phebe said, 'Won't you please give me an apple?' and Deb said, 'Drat you! No, I won't!' My mother wasn't afraid, so she took an apple for Phebe and one for herself, and she said to Deb:—

"'I ain't afraid of ye, ye old witch!'

"'Ye ain't?' Deb screamed; 'then I'll make ye afraid afore ye git home!'

"They had a piece of woods to go through; in the middle of it there was a pair of bars, and on the other side of the bars there was a brook. Suddenly they heard a roaring and they saw a black bull coming. 'Oh!' said Phebe, 'Captain Besse's bull has got out and he will get us'; so they ran for the bars. They got through them and across the brook, when the bull leaped the bars and stopped on the edge of the brook and roared; then my mother knew it was old Deb Burden who was in the bull to frighten the girls, because the brook stopped the critter. Witches can't cross running water, you know.

"The girls reached home dreadfully frightened, and told what had happened. 'Never mind,' said my grandfather; 'I'll fix Debbie!' When she brought home the cloth, he came into the house and slipped behind her as she sat by the fire, and put a darning-needle through her dress and fastened her to the chair. Well, she sot; and every once in a while she said, 'I must go'; but she couldn't stir; she would be still for a while and then say, 'Why, I must go and tend my fire'; but she couldn't stir no more'n a milestone; and he kept her in the chair all day, and then he pulled out the needle and let her go. 'Scare my gal agin, ye old witch!' he said. You know witches can't do anything when steel is nigh, and that was the reason the darning-needle held her.

"Once Deb came to Thankful Haskell's in Rochester, and sot by the fire, and her daughter, fourteen year old, was sweeping the room, and she put the broom under Deb's chair. You can't insult a witch more than that, 'cause a broomstick is what they ride on when they go off on mischief. Deb was mad as a March hare, and she cussed the child. Next day the child was taken sick, and all the doctors gin her up, and they sent for old Dr. Bemis of Middleboro; he put on his spectacles and looked at her, and said he, 'This child is bewitched; go, somebody, and see what Deb is up to.' Mr. Haskell got on his horse and rode to Deb's house; there was nobody in but a big black cat; this was the devil, and witches always leave him to take care of the house when they go out. Mr. Haskell looked around for Deb, and he saw her down to the bottom of the garden by a pool of water, and she was making images out of clay and sticking in pins. As quick as he saw her he knew what ailed the child; so he laid his whip around her shoulders good, and said, 'Stop that, Deb, or you shall be burnt alive!' She whimpered, and the black cat came out and growled and spread his tail, but Mr. Haskell laid on the whip, and at last she screamed, 'Your young one shall git well!' and that child began to mend right off. The black cat disappeared all of a suddint and Mr. Haskell thought the earth opened and took him in."

"Moll Ellis was called the witch of Plymouth," said the other sister, taking up the story-telling. "She got a grudge agin Mr. Stevens, a man my grandfather worked for, and three years runnin' she cast a spell on the cattle and horses, and upsot his hay in a brook. My grandfather drove and Stevens was on the load, and when they came to the brook the oxen snorted, and the horses reared and sweat, and they all backed and the hay was upsot into the brook. One day Stevens said, 'I'll not stand this; I'll go and see what Moll Ellis is about.' So he went up to her house, and there she lay on her back a-chewin' and a-mutterin' dretful spell words, and as quick as Stevens saw her he knew what ailed his cattle; and he walked right up to the bed, and he told Moll, 'If you ever upset another load of hay I'll have you hung for a witch.' She was dretful scart, and promised she never would harm him again. When she was talking, a little black devil, that looked just like a bumblebee, flew into the window and popped down her throat; 't was the one she had sent out to scare the cattle and horses. When Moll died, they couldn't get the coffin out the door because it had a steel latch; they had to put it out the window."

The Wraith in the Storm

[SAMUEL ADAMS DRAKE]

The number of persons who have testified to having seen the apparitions or death wraiths of dying or deceased friends is already large, as the records of various societies for psychical research bear witness. These phenomena are not in their nature forewarnings of something that is about to happen, but announcements of something that already has happened. They therefore can have no relation to what was formerly known as "second sight."

In spite of all that our much-boasted civilization has done in the way of freeing poor, fallible man from the thraldom of superstition, there is indubitable evidence that a great many people still put faith in direct revelations from the land of spirits. In the course of a quiet chat one evening, where the subject was under discussion, one of the company who had listened attentively, though silently all the while, to all manner of theories, spiced with ridicule, abruptly asked how we would account for the following incident which he went on to relate, and I have here set down word for word:—

"My grandparents," he began, "had a son whom they thought all the world of. From all accounts I guess Tom was about one of the likeliest young fellows that could be scared up in a day's journey. Everybody said Tom was bound to make his mark in the world, and at the time I speak of he seemed in a fair way of doing it, too, for at one and twenty he was first mate of the old *Argonaut* which had just sailed for Calcutta. This would make her tenth voyage. Well, as I am telling you, the very day after the *Argonaut* went to sea, a tremendous gale set in from the eastward. It blew great guns. Actually, now, it seemed as if that gale would never stop blowing.

"As day after day went by, and the storm raged on without intermission, you may judge if the hearts of those who had friends at sea in that ship did not sink down and down with the passing hours. Of course, the old folks could think of nothing else.

"Let me see; it was a good bit ago. Ah, yes; it was on the third or fourth night of the gale, I don't rightly remember which, and it don't matter much, that grandfather and grandmother were sitting together, as usual, in the old family sitting-

room, he poring over the family Bible as he was
wont to do in such cases, she knitting and rocking,
or pretending to knit, but both full of the one ever
present thought, which each was trying so hard to
hide from the other.

"Dismally splashed the raindrops against the
windowpanes, mournfully the wind whined in the
chimney-top, while every now and then the fire
would spit and sputter angrily on the hearth, or
flare up fitfully when some big gust came roaring
down the chimney to fan the embers into a fiercer
flame. Then there would be a lull, during which,
like an echo of the tempest, the dull and distant
booming of the sea was borne to the affrighted
listener's ears. But nothing I could say would begin
to give you an idea of the great gale of 1817.

"Well, the old folks sat there as stiff as two statues,
listening to every sound. When a big gust tore over
the house and shook it till it rocked again, gran'ther
would steal a look at grandmother over his specs,
but say never a word. The old lady would give a
start, let her hands fall idly upon her lap, sit for a
moment as if dazed, and then go on with her knitting again as if her very life depended on it.

"Unable at length to control her feelings, grandmother got up out of her chair, with her work in
her hand, went to the window, put aside the curtain,
and looked out. I say looked out, for of course all
was so pitchdark outside that nothing could be

seen, yet there she stood with her white face pressed close to the wet panes, peering out into the night, as if questioning the storm itself of the absent one.

"All at once she drew back from the window with a low cry, saying in a broken voice: 'My God, father, it's Tom in his coffin! They're bringing him up here, to the house.' Then she covered her face with her hands, to shut out the horrid sight.

" 'Set down 'Mandy!' sternly commanded the startled old man. 'Don't be making a fool of yourself. Don't ye know tain't no sech a thing what you're saying? Set down, I say, this minnit!'

"But no one could ever convince grandmother that she had not actually seen, with her own eyes, her dear boy Tom, the idol of her heart, lying cold in death. To her indeed it was a revelation from the tomb, for the ship in which Tom had sailed was never heard from."

Jonathan Moulton
and the Devil

[SAMUEL ADAMS DRAKE]

The legendary hero of Hampton is General Jonathan Moulton. He is no fictitious personage, but one of veritable flesh and blood, who, having acquired considerably celebrity in the old wars, lives on through the medium of a local legend.

The General, says the legend, encountered a far more notable adversary than Abenaki warriors or conjurers, among whom he had lived, and whom it was the passion of his life to exterminate.

In an evil hour his yearning to amass wealth suddenly led him to declare that he would sell his soul for the possession of unbounded riches. Think of the Devil, and he is at your elbow. The fatal declaration was no sooner made—the General was sitting alone by his fireside—than a shower of sparks came down the chimney, out of which stepped a man dressed from top to toe in black velvet. The astonished Moulton noticed that the stranger's ruffles were not even smutted.

"Your servant, General!" quoth the stranger, suavely. "But let us make haste, if you please, for I am expected at the Governor's in a quarter of an hour," he added, picking up a live coal with his thumb and forefinger, and consulting his watch with it.

The General's wits began to desert him. Portsmouth was five leagues—long ones at that—from Hampton House, and his strange visitor talked, with the utmost unconcern, of getting there in fifteen minutes! His astonishment caused him to stammer out,—

"Then you must be the—"

"Tush! what signifies a name?" interrupted the stranger, with a deprecating wave of the hand. "Come, do we understand each other? Is it a bargain, or not?"

At the talismanic word "bargain" the General pricked up his ears. He had often been heard to say that neither man nor devil could get the better of him in a trade. He took out his jack-knife and began to whittle. The Devil took out his, and began to pare his nails.

"But what proof have I that you can perform what you promise?" demanded Moulton, pursing up his mouth and contracting his bushy eyebrows, like a man who is not to be taken in by mere appearances.

The fiend ran his fingers carelessly through his peruke, when a shower of golden guineas fell to the floor and rolled to the four corners of the room. The General quickly stopped to pick up one; but no sooner had his fingers closed upon it, than he dropped it with a yell. It was red-hot!

The Devil chuckled; "Try again," he said. But Moulton shook his head and retreated a step.

"Don't be afraid."

Moulton cautiously touched a coin; it was cool. He weighed it in his hand, and rung it on the table; it was full weight and true ring. Then he went down on his hands and knees, and began to gather up the guineas with feverish haste.

"Are you satisfied?" demanded Satan.

"Completely, your Majesty."

"Then to business. By the way, have you anything to drink in the house?"

"There is some Old Jamaica in the cupboard."

"Excellent! I am as thirsty as a Puritan on election-day," said the Devil, seating himself at the table, and negligently flinging his mantle back over his shoulder, so as to show the jewelled clasps of his doublet.

Moulton brought a decanter and a couple of glasses from the cupboard, filled one, and passed it to his infernal guest, who tasted it, and smacked his lips with the air of a connoisseur. Moulton watched every gesture.

"Does your Excellency not find it to your taste?" he ventured to ask; having the secret idea that he might get the Devil drunk, and so outwit him.

"H'm, I have drunk worse. But let me show you how to make a salamander," replied Satan, touching the lighted end of the taper to the liquor, which instantly burst into a spectral blue flame. The fiend then raised the tankard to the height of his eye, glanced approvingly at the blaze,—which to Moulton's disordered intellect resembled an adder's forked and agile tongue,—nodded, and said, patronizingly, "To our better acquaintance!" He then quaffed the contents at a single gulp.

Moulton shuddered; this was not the way he had been used to seeing healths drunk. He pretended, however, to drink, for fear of giving offence; but somehow the liquor choked him. The demon set down the tankard, and observed, in a matter-of-fact way that put his listener in a cold sweat: "Now that you are convinced I am able to make you the richest man in all the province, listen! Have I your ear? It is well! In consideration of your agreement, duly signed and sealed, to deliver your soul"—here he drew a parchment from his breast—"I engage, on my part, on the first day of every month, to fill your boots with golden elephants, like these before you. But mark me well," said Satan, holding up a forefinger glittering with diamonds, "if you try to play me any trick, you will repent it! I know you, Jonathan Moulton, and shall keep my eye upon you; so beware!"

Moulton flinched a little at this plain speech; but a thought seemed to strike him, and he brightened up. Satan opened the scroll, smoothed out the creases, dipped a pen in the inkhorn at his girdle, and pointing to a blank space, said, laconically, "Sign!"

Moulton hesitated.

"If you are afraid," sneered Satan, "why put me to all this trouble?" and he began to put the gold in his pocket.

His victim seized the pen; but his hand shook so that he could not write. He gulped down a mouthful of rum, stole a look at his infernal guest, who nodded his head by way of encouragement, and a second time approached his pen to the paper. The struggle was soon over. The unhappy Moulton wrote his name at the bottom of the fatal list, which he was astonished to see numbered some of the highest personages in the province. "I shall at least be in good company," he muttered.

"Good!" said Satan, rising and putting the scroll carefully away within his breast. "Rely on me, General, and be sure you keep faith. Remember!" So saying, the demon waved his hand, flung his mantle about him, and vanished up the chimney.

Satan performed his part of the contract to the letter. On the first day of every month the boots, which were hung on the crane in the fireplace the night before, were found in the morning stuffed full of guineas. It is true that Moulton had ransacked the village for the largest pair to be found, and had finally secured a brace of trooper's jack-boots, which came nearly up to the wearer's thigh; but the contract merely expressed boots, and the Devil does not stand upon trifles.

Moulton rolled in wealth; everything prospered. His neighbors regarded him first with envy, then with aversion, at last with fear. Not a few affirmed that he had entered into a league with the Evil One. Others shook their heads, saying, "What does it signify?—that man would outwit the Devil himself."

But one morning, when the fiend came as usual to fill the boots, what was his astonishment to find that he could not fill them. He poured in the guineas, but it was like pouring water into a rat-hole. The more he put in, the more the quantity seemed to diminish. In vain he persisted; the boots could not be filled.

The Devil scratched his ear. "I must look into this," he reflected. No sooner said, than he attempted to descend; but in doing so he found his progress suddenly stopped. A good reason. The chimney was choked up with guineas! Foaming with rage, the demon tore the boots from the crane. The crafty

General had cut off the soles, leaving only the legs for the Devil to fill. The chamber was knee-deep with gold.

The Devil gave a horrible grin, and disappeared. The same night Hampton House was burned to the ground, the General only escaping in his shirt. He had been dreaming he was dead and in hell. His precious guineas were secreted in the wainscot, the ceiling, and other hiding-places known only to himself. He blasphemed, wept, and tore his hair. Suddenly he grew calm. After all, the loss was not irreparable, he reflected. Gold would melt, it is true; but he would find it all,—of course he would,—at daybreak, run into a solid lump in the cellar,— every guinea. That is true of ordinary gold.

The General worked with the energy of despair, clearing away the rubbish. He refused all offers of assistance; he dared not accept them. But the gold had vanished. Whether it was really consumed, or had passed again into the massy entrails of the earth, will never be known. It is only certain that every vestige of it had disappeared.

When the General died and was buried, strange rumors began to circulate. To quiet them, the grave was opened; but when the lid was removed from the coffin, it was found to be empty.

Another legend runs to the effect that upon the death of his wife under—as evil report would have it—very suspicious circumstances, the General paid his court to a young woman who had been the companion of his deceased spouse. They were married. In the middle of the night the young bride awoke with a start. She felt an invisible hand trying to take off from her finger the wedding-ring that had once belonged to the dead and buried Mrs. Moulton. Shrieking with fright, she jumped out of bed, thus awaking her husband; who tried in vain to calm her fears. Candles were lighted and search made for the ring; but as it could never be found again, the ghostly visitor was supposed to have carried it away with her. This story is the same that is told by Whittier in the "New Wife and the Old."

From The Spouter-Inn to Nantucket

[HERMAN MELVILLE]

THE SPOUTER-INN

Entering that gable-ended Spouter-Inn, you found yourself in a wide, low, straggling entry with old-fashioned wainscots, reminding one of the bulwarks of some condemned old craft. On one side hung a very large oil-painting so thoroughly be-smoked, and every way defaced, that in the unequal cross-lights by which you viewed it, it was only by diligent study and a series of systematic visits to it, and careful inquiry of the neighbors, that you could any way arrive at an understanding of its purpose. Such unaccountable masses of shades and shadows, that at first you almost thought some ambitious young artist, in the time of the New England hags, had endeavored to delineate chaos bewitched. But by dint of much and earnest contemplation, and oft repeated ponderings, and especially by throwing open the little window towards the back of the entry, you at last came to the conclusion that such an idea, however wild, might not be altogether unwarranted.

But what most puzzled and confounded you was a long, limber, portentous, black mass of something hovering in the centre of the picture over three blue, dim, perpendicular lines floating in a nameless yeast. A boggy, soggy, squitchy picture truly, enough to drive a nervous man distracted. Yet was there a sort of indefinite, half-attained, unimaginable sublimity about it that fairly froze you to it, till you involuntarily took an oath with yourself to find out what that marvellous painting meant. Ever and anon a bright, but, alas, deceptive idea would dart you through.— It's the Black Sea in a midnight gale.—It's the unnatural combat of the four primal elements.—It's a blasted heath.—It's a Hyperborean winter scene.— It's the breaking-up of the ice-bound stream of Time. But at last all these fancies yielded to that one portentous something in the picture's midst. *That* once found out, and all the rest were plain. But stop; does it not bear a faint resemblance to a gigantic fish? even the great leviathan himself?

In fact, the artist's design seemed this: a final theory of my own, partly based upon the aggregated opinions of many aged persons with whom I conversed upon the subject. The picture represents a

Cape-Horner in a great hurricane; the half-founded ship weltering there with its three dismantled masts alone visible; and an exasperated whale, purposing to spring clean over the craft, is in the enormous act of impaling himself upon the three mast-heads.

The opposite wall of this entry was hung all over with a heathenish array of monstrous clubs and spears. Some were thickly set with glittering teeth resembling ivory saws; others were tufted with knots of human hair; and one was sickle-shaped, with a vast handle sweeping round like the segment made in the new-mown grass by a long-armed mower. You shuddered as you gazed, and wondered what monstrous cannibal and savage could ever have gone a death-harvesting with such a hacking, horrifying implement. Mixed with these were rusty old whaling lances and harpoons all broken and deformed. Some were storied weapons. With this once long lance, now wildly elbowed, fifty years ago did Nathan Swain kill fifteen whales between a sunrise and a sunset. And that harpoon—so like a corkscrew now—was flung in Javan seas, and run away with by a whale, years afterwards slain off the Cape of Blanco. The original iron entered nigh the tail, and, like a restless needle sojourning in the body of a man, travelled full forty feet, and at last was found imbedded in the hump.

Crossing this dusky entry, and on through yon low-arched way—cut through what in old times must have been a great central chimney with fire-places all round—you enter the public room. A still duskier place is this, with such low ponderous beams above, and such old wrinkled planks beneath, that you would almost fancy you trod some old craft's cockpits, especially of such a howling night, when this corner-anchored old ark rocked so furiously. On one side stood a long, low, shelf-like table covered with cracked glass cases, filled with dusty rarities gathered from this wide world's remotest nooks. Projecting from the further angle of the room stands a dark-looking den—the bar—a rude attempt at a right whale's head. Be that how it may, there stands the vast arched bone of the whale's jaw, so wide, a coach might almost drive beneath it. Within are shabby shelves, ranged round with old decanters, bottles, flasks; and in those jaws of swift destruction, like another cursed Jonah (by which name indeed they called him), bustles a little withered old man, who, for their money, dearly sells the sailors deliri-ums and death.

Abominable are the tumblers into which he pours his poison. Though true cylinders with-out—within, the villanous green goggling glasses deceitfully tapered downwards to a cheating bot-tom. Parallel meridians rudely pecked into the glass, surround these footpads' goblets. Fill to *this* mark, and your charge is but a penny; to *this* a penny more; and so on to the full glass—the Cape Horn measure, which you may gulp down for a shilling.

Upon entering the place I found a number of young seamen gathered about a table, examining by a dim light divers specimens of *skrimshander*. I sought the landlord, and telling him I desired to be accommodated with a room, received for answer that his house was full—not a bed unoccupied. "But avast," he added, tapping his forehead, "you haint no objections to sharing a harpooneer's blanket, have ye? I s'pose you are goin' a whalin', so you'd better get used to that sort of thing."

I told him that I never liked to sleep two in a bed; that if I should ever do so, it would depend upon who the harpooneer might be, and that if he (the landlord) really had no other place for me, and the harpooneer was not decidedly objectionable, why rather than wander further about a strange town on so bitter a night, I would put up with the half of any decent man's blanket.

"I thought so. All right; take a seat. Supper?—you want supper? Supper 'll be ready directly."

I sat down on an old wooden settle, carved all over like a bench on the Battery. At one end a ruminating tar was still further adorning it with his jackknife, stooping over and diligently working away at the space between his legs. He was trying his hand at a ship under full sail, but he didn't make much headway, I thought.

At last some four or five of us were summoned to our meal in an adjoining room. It was cold as Iceland—no fire at all—the landlord said he couldn't afford it. Nothing but two dismal tallow candles, each in a winding sheet. We were fain to button up our monkey jackets, and hold to our lips cups of scalding tea with our half frozen fingers. But the fare was of the most substantial kind—not only meat and potatoes, but dumplings; good heavens! dumplings for supper! One young fellow in a green box coat, addressed himself to these dumplings in a most direful manner.

"My boy," said the landlord, "you'll have the nightmare to a dead sartainty."

"Landlord," I whispered, "that aint the harpooneer, is it?"

"Oh, no," said he, looking a sort of diabolically funny, "the harpooneer is a dark complexioned chap. He never eats dumplings, he don't—he eats nothing but steaks, and likes 'em rare."

"The devil he does," says I. "Where is that harpooneer? Is he here?"

"He'll be here afore long," was the answer.

I could not help it, but I began to feel suspicious of this "dark complexioned" harpooneer. At any rate, I made up my mind that if it so turned out that we should sleep together, he must undress and get into bed before I did.

Supper over, the company went back to the bar-room, when, knowing not what else to do with myself, I resolved to spend the rest of the evening as a looker on.

Presently a rioting noise was heard without. Starting up, the landlord cried, "That's the Grampus's crew. I seed her reported in the offing this morning; a three years' voyage, and a full ship. Hurrah, boys; now we'll have the latest news from the Feegees."

A tramping of sea boots was heard in the entry; the door was flung open, and in rolled a wild set of mariners enough. Enveloped in their shaggy watch coats, and with their heads muffled in woollen comforters, all bedarned and ragged, and their beards stiff with icicles, they seemed an eruption of bears from Labrador. They had just landed from their boat, and this was the first house they entered. No wonder, then, that they made a straight wake for the whale's mouth—the bar—when the wrinkled little old Jonah, there officiating, soon poured them out brimmers all round. One complained of a bad cold in his head, upon which Jonah mixed him a pitch-like potion of gin and molasses, which he swore was a sovereign cure for all colds and catarrhs whatsoever, never mind of how long standing, or whether caught off the coast of Labrador, or on the weather side of an ice-island.

The liquor soon mounted into their heads, as it generally does even with the arrantest topers newly landed from sea, and they began capering about most obstreperously.

I observed, however, that one of them held somewhat aloof, and though he seemed desirous not to spoil the hilarity of his shipmates by his own sober face, yet upon the whole he refrained from making as much noise as the rest. This man interested me at once; and since the sea-gods had ordained that he should soon become my shipmate (though but a sleeping-partner one, so far as this narrative is concerned), I will here venture upon a little description of him. He stood full six feet in height, with noble shoulders, and a chest like a coffer-dam. I have seldom seen such brawn in a man. His face was deeply brown and burnt, making his white teeth dazzling by the contrast; while in the deep shadows of his eyes floated some reminiscences that did not seem to give him much joy. His voice at once announced that he was a Southerner, and from his fine stature, I thought he must be one of those tall mountaineers from the Alleghanian Ridge in Virginia. When the revelry of his companions had mounted to its height, this man slipped away unobserved, and I saw no more of him till he became my comrade on the sea. In a few minutes, however, he was missed by his shipmates, and being, it seems, for some reason a huge favorite with

them, they raised a cry of "Bulkington! Bulkington! where's Bulkington?" and darted out of the
house in pursuit of him.

It was now about nine o'clock, and the room
seeming almost supernaturally quiet after these
orgies, I began to congratulate myself upon a little
plan that had occurred to me just previous to the
entrance of the seamen.

No man prefers to sleep two in a bed. In fact, you
would a good deal rather not sleep with your own
brother. I don't know how it is, but people like to
be private when they are sleeping. And when it
comes to sleeping with an unknown stranger, in a
strange inn, in a strange town, and that stranger a
harpooneer, then your objections indefinitely
multiply. Nor was there any earthly reason why I as
a sailor should sleep two in a bed, more than anybody else; for sailors no more sleep two in a bed at
sea, than bachelor Kings do ashore. To be sure they
all sleep together in one apartment, but you have
your own hammock, and cover yourself with your
own blanket, and sleep in your own skin.

The more I pondered over this harpooneer, the
more I abominated the thought of sleeping with
him. It was fair to presume that being a harpooneer,
his linen or woollen, as the case might be, would
not be of the tidiest, certainly none of the finest. I
began to twitch all over. Besides, it was getting late,
and any decent harpooneer ought to be home and

going bed-wards. Suppose now, he should tumble in upon me at midnight—how could I tell from what vile hole he had been coming?

"Landlord! I've changed my mind about that harpooneer.—I shan't sleep with him. I'll try the bench here."

"Just as you please; I'm sorry I cant spare ye a table-cloth for a mattress, and it's a plaguy rough board here"—feeling of the knots and notches. "But wait a bit, Skrimshander; I've got a carpenter's plane there in the bar—wait, I say, and I'll make ye snug enough." So saying he procured the plane; and with his old silk handkerchief first dusting the bench, vigorously set to planing away at my bed, the while grinning like an ape. The shavings flew right and left; till at last the plane-iron came bump against an indestructible knot. The landlord was near spraining his wrist, and I told him for heaven's sake to quit—the bed was soft enough to suit me, and I did not know how all the planing in the world could make eider down of a pine plank. So gathering up the shavings with another grin, and throwing them into the great stove in the middle of the room, he went about his business, and left me in a brown study.

I now took the measure of the bench, and found that it was a foot too short; but that could be mended with a chair. But it was a foot too narrow, and the other bench in the room was about four inches higher than the planed one—so there was no yoking them. I then placed the first bench lengthwise along the only clear space against the wall, leaving a little interval between, for my back to settle down in. But I soon found that there came such a draught of cold air over me from under the sill of the window, that this plan would never do at all, especially as another current from the rickety door met the one from the window, and both together formed a series of small whirlwinds in the immediate vicinity of the spot where I had thought to spend the night.

The devil fetch that harpooneer, thought I, but stop, couldn't I steal a march on him—bolt his door inside, and jump into his bed, not to be wakened by the most violent knockings? It seemed no bad idea; but upon second thoughts I dismissed it. For who could tell but what the next morning, so soon as I popped out of the room, the harpooneer might be standing in the entry, all ready to knock me down!

Still, looking round me again, and seeing no possible chance of spending a sufferable night unless in some other person's bed, I began to think that after all I might be cherishing unwarrantable prejudices against this unknown harpooneer. Thinks I, I'll wait awhile; he must be dropping in before long. I'll have a good look at him then, and perhaps we may become jolly good bedfellows after all—there's no telling.

But though the other boarders kept coming in by ones, twos, and threes, and going to bed, yet no sign of my harpooneer.

"Landlord!" said I, "what sort of a chap is he—does he always keep such late hours?" It was now hard upon twelve o'clock.

The landlord chuckled again with his lean chuckle, and seemed to be mightily tickled at something beyond my comprehension. "No," he answered, "generally he's an airley bird—airley to bed and airley to rise—yes, he's the bird what catches the worm.—But to-night he went out a peddling, you see, and I don't see what on airth keeps him so late, unless, may be, he can't sell his head."

"Can't sell his head?—What sort of a bamboo-zling story is this you are telling me?" getting into a towering rage. "Do you pretend to say, landlord, that this harpooneer is actually engaged this blessed Saturday night, or rather Sunday morning, in ped-dling his head around this town?"

"That's precisely it," said the landlord, "and I told him he couldn't sell it here, the market's over-stocked."

"With what?" shouted I.

"With heads to be sure; ain't there too many heads in the world?"

"I tell you what it is, landlord," said I, quite calmly, "you'd better stop spinning that yarn to me—I'm not green."

"May be not," taking out a stick and whittling a toothpick, "but I rayther guess you'll be done *brown* if that ere harpooneer hears you a slanderin his head."

"I'll break it for him," said I, now flying into a passion again at this unaccountable farrago of the landlord's.

"It's broke a'ready," said he.

"Broke," said I—"*broke,* do you mean?"

"Sartain, and that's the very reason he can't sell it, I guess."

"Landlord," said I, going up to him as cool as Mt. Hecla in a snow storm—"landlord, stop whittling. You and I must understand one another, and that too without delay. I come to your house and want a bed; you tell me you can only give me half a one; that the other half belongs to a certain harpooneer. And about this harpooneer, whom I have not yet seen, you persist in telling me the most mystifying and exasperating stories, tending to beget in me an uncomfortable feeling towards the man whom you design for my bedfellow—a sort of connexion, landlord, which is an intimate and confidential one in the highest degree. I now demand of you to speak out and tell me who and what this harpooneer is, and whether I shall be in all respects safe to spend the night with him. And in the first place, you will be so good as to unsay that story about selling his head, which if true I take to be good evidence that this harpooneer is stark mad, and I've no idea of sleeping with a madman; and you, sir, *you* I mean, landlord, *you*, sir, by trying to induce me to do so knowingly, would thereby render yourself liable to a criminal prosecution."

"Wall," said the landlord, fetching a long breath, "that's a purty long sarmon for a chap that rips a little now and then. But be easy, be easy, this here harpooneer I have been tellin' you of has just arrived from the south seas, where he bought up a lot of 'balmed New Zealand heads (great curios, you know), and he's sold all on 'em but one, and that one he's trying to sell to-night, cause to-morrow's Sunday, and it would not do to be sellin' human heads about the streets when folks is goin' to churches. He wanted to, last Sunday, but I stopped him just as he was goin' out of the door with four heads strung on a string, for all the airth like a string of onions."

This account cleared up the otherwise unaccountable mystery, and showed that the landlord, after all, had had no idea of fooling me—but at the same time what could I think of a harpooneer who stayed out of a Saturday night clean into the holy Sabbath, engaged in such a cannibal business as selling the heads of dead idolators?

"Depend upon it, landlord, that harpooneer is a dangerous man."

"He pays reg'lar," was the rejoinder. "But come, it's getting dreadful late, you had better be turning flukes—it's a nice bed: Sal and me slept in that ere bed the night we were spliced. There's plenty room for two to kick about in that bed; it's an almighty big bed that. Why, afore we give it up, Sal used to put our Sam and little Johnny in the foot of it. But I got a dreaming and sprawling about one night, and somehow, Sam got pitched on the floor, and came near breaking his arm. Arter that, Sal said it wouldn't do. Come along here, I'll give ye a glim in a jiffy;" and so saying he lighted a candle and held it towards me, offering to lead the way. But I stood irresolute; when looking at a clock in the corner, he exclaimed, "I vum it's Sunday—you won't see that harpooneer to-night; he's come to anchor some-where—come along then; *do* come; *won't* ye come?"

I considered the matter a moment, and then up stairs we went, and I was ushered into a small room, cold as a clam, and furnished, sure enough, with a prodigious bed, almost big enough indeed for any four harpooneers to sleep abreast.

"There," said the landlord, placing the candle on a crazy old sea chest that did double duty as a wash-stand and centre table; "there, make yourself com-fortable now, and good night to ye." I turned round from eyeing the bed, but he had disappeared.

Folding back the counterpane, I stooped over the bed. Though none of the most elegant, it yet stood the scrutiny tolerably well. I then glanced round the room; and besides the bedstead and centre table, could see no other furniture belonging to the place, but a rude shelf, the four walls, and a papered fire-board representing a man striking a whale. Of things not properly belonging to the room, there was a hammock lashed up, and thrown upon the floor in one corner; also a large seaman's bag, containing the harpooneer's wardrobe, no doubt in lieu of a land trunk. Likewise, there was a parcel of outlandish bone fish hooks on the shelf over the fire-place, and a tall harpoon standing at the head of the bed.

But what is this on the chest? I took it up, and held it close to the light, and felt it, and smelt it, and tried every way possible to arrive at some satisfactory conclusion concerning it. I can compare it to nothing but a large door mat, ornamented at the edges with little tinkling tags something like the stained porcupine quills round an Indian moccasin. There was a hole or slit in the middle of this mat, the same as in South American ponchos. But could it be possible that any sober harpooneer would get into a door mat, and parade the streets of any Christian town in that sort of guise? I put it on, to try it, and it weighed me down like a hamper, being uncommonly shaggy and thick, and I thought a little damp, as though this mysterious harpooneer had been wearing it of a rainy day. I went up in it to a bit of glass stuck against the wall, and I never saw such a sight in my life. I tore myself out of it in such a hurry that I gave myself a kink in the neck.

I sat down on the side of the bed, and commenced thinking about this head-peddling harpooneer, and his door mat. After thinking some time on the bed-side, I got up and took off my monkey jacket, and then stood in the middle of the room thinking. I then took off my coat, and thought a little more in my shirt sleeves. But beginning to feel very cold now, half undressed as I was, and remembering what the landlord said about the harpooneer's not coming home at all that night, it being so very late, I made no more ado, but jumped out of my pantaloons and boots, and then blowing out the light tumbled into bed, and commended myself to the care of heaven.

Whether that mattress was stuffed with corn-cobs or broken crockery, there is no telling, but I rolled about a good deal, and could not sleep for a long time. At last I slid off into a light doze, and had pretty nearly made a good offing towards the land of Nod, when I heard a heavy footfall in the passage, and saw a glimmer of light come into the room from under the door.

Lord save me, thinks I, that must be the harpooneer, the infernal head-peddler. But I lay perfectly still, and resolved not to say a word till spoken to. Holding a light in one hand, and that identical New Zealand head in the other, the stranger entered the room, and without looking towards the bed, placed his candle a good way off from me on the floor in one corner, and then began working away at the knotted cords of the large bag I before spoke of as being in the room. I was all eagerness to see his face, but he kept it averted for some time while employed in unlacing the bag's mouth. This accomplished, however, he turned round—when, good heavens! what a sight! Such a face! It was of a dark, purplish, yellow color, here and there stuck over with large, blackish looking squares. Yes, it's just as I thought, he's a terrible bedfellow; he's been in a fight, got dreadfully cut, and here he is, just from the surgeon. But at that moment he chanced to turn his face so towards the light, that I plainly saw they could not be sticking-plasters at all, those black squares on his cheeks. They were stains of some sort or other. At first I knew not what to make of this; but soon an inkling of the truth occurred to me. I remembered a story of a white man—a whaleman too—who, falling among the cannibals, had been tattooed by them. I concluded that this harpooneer, in the course of his distant voyages, must have met with a similar adventure. And what is it, thought I, after all! It's only his outside; a man can be honest in any sort of skin. But then, what to make of his unearthly complexion, that part of it, I mean, lying round about, and completely independent of the squares of tattooing. To be sure, it might be nothing but a good coat of tropical tanning; but I never heard of a hot sun's tanning a white man into a purplish yellow one. However, I had never been in the South Seas; and perhaps the sun there produced these extraordinary effects upon the skin. Now, while all these ideas were passing through me like lightning, this harpooneer never noticed me at all. But, after some difficulty having opened his bag, he commenced fumbling in it, and presently pulled out a sort of tomahawk, and a seal-skin wallet with the hair on. Placing these on the old chest in the middle of the room, he then took the New Zealand head— a ghastly thing enough—and crammed it down into the bag. He now took off his hat—a new beaver hat—when I came nigh singing out with fresh surprise. There was no hair on his head—none to speak of at least—nothing but a small scalp-knot twisted up on his forehead. His bald purplish head now looked for all the world like a mildewed skull. Had not the stranger stood between me and the door, I would have bolted out of it quicker than ever I bolted a dinner.

Even as it was, I thought something of slipping out of the window, but it was the second floor back. I am no coward, but what to make of this head-peddling purple rascal altogether passed my comprehension. Ignorance is the parent of fear, and being completely nonplussed and confounded about the stranger, I confess I was now as much afraid of him as if it was the devil himself who had thus broken into my room at the dead of night. In fact, I was so afraid of him that I was not game enough just then to address him, and demand a satisfactory answer concerning what seemed inexplicable in him.

Meanwhile, he continued the business of undressing, and at last showed his chest and arms. As I live, these covered parts of him were checkered with the same squares as his face; his back, too, was all over the same dark squares; he seemed to have been in a Thirty Years' War, and just escaped from it with a sticking-plaster shirt. Still more, his very legs were marked, as if a parcel of dark green frogs were running up the trunks of young palms. It was now quite plain that he must be some abominable savage or other shipped aboard of a whaleman in the South Seas, and so landed in this Christian country. I quaked to think of it. A peddler of heads too—perhaps the heads of his own brothers. He might take a fancy to mine—heavens! look at that tomahawk!

But there was no time for shuddering, for now the savage went about something that completely fascinated my attention, and convinced me that he must indeed be a heathen. Going to his heavy grego, or wrapall, or dreadnaught, which he had previously hung on a chair, he fumbled in the pockets, and produced at length a curious little deformed image with a hunch on its back, and exactly the color of a three days' old Congo baby. Remembering the embalmed head, at first I almost thought that this black manikin was a real baby preserved in some

similar manner. But seeing that it was not at all limber, and that it glistened a good deal like polished
ebony, I concluded that it must be nothing but a
wooden idol, which indeed it proved to be. For
now the savage goes up to the empty fire-place, and
removing the papered fire-board, sets up this little hunchbacked image, like a tenpin, between
the andirons. The chimney jambs and all the bricks
inside were very sooty, so that I thought this fire-
place made a very appropriate little shrine or chapel
for his Congo idol.

I now screwed my eyes hard towards the half
hidden image, feeling but ill at ease meantime—to
see what was next to follow. First he takes about a
double handful of shavings out of his grego
pocket, and places them carefully before the idol;
then laying a bit of ship biscuit on top and apply-
ing the flame from the lamp, he kindled the shavings into a sacrificial blaze. Presently, after many
hasty snatches into the fire, and still hastier with-
drawals of his fingers (whereby he seemed to be
scorching them badly), he at last succeeded in
drawing out the biscuit; then blowing off the heat
and ashes a little, he made a polite offer of it to the
little negro. But the little devil did not seem to
fancy such dry sort of fare at all; he never moved
his lips. All these strange antics were accompanied
by still stranger guttural noises from the devotee,
who seemed to be praying in a sing-song or else

singing some pagan psalmody or other, during which his face twitched about in the most unnatural manner. At last extinguishing the fire, he took the idol up very unceremoniously, and bagged it again in his grego pocket as carelessly as if he were a sportsman bagging a dead woodcock.

All these queer proceedings increased my uncomfortableness, and seeing him now exhibiting strong symptoms of concluding his business operations, and jumping into bed with me, I thought it was high time, now or never, before the light was put out, to break the spell in which I had so long been bound.

But the interval I spent in deliberating what to say, was a fatal one. Taking up his tomahawk from the table, he examined the head of it for an instant, and then holding it to the light, with his mouth at the handle, he puffed out great clouds of tobacco smoke. The next moment the light was extinguished, and this wild cannibal, tomahawk between his teeth, sprang into bed with me. I sang out, I could not help it now; and giving a sudden grunt of astonishment he began feeling me.

Stammering out something, I knew not what, I rolled away from him against the wall, and then conjured him, whoever or whatever he might be, to keep quiet, and let me get up and light the lamp again. But his guttural responses satisfied me at once that he but ill comprehended my meaning.

"Who-e debel you?"—he at last said—"you no speak-e, dam-me, I kill-e." And so saying the lighted tomahawk began flourishing about me in the dark.

"Landlord, for God's sake, Peter Coffin!" shouted I. "Landlord! Watch! Coffin! Angels! save me!"

"Speak-e! tell-ee me who-ee be, or dam-me, I kill-e!" again growled the cannibal, while his horrid flourishings of the tomahawk scattered the hot tobacco ashes about me till I thought my linen would get on fire. But thank heaven, at that moment the landlord came into the room light in hand, and leaping from the bed I ran up to him.

"Don't be afraid now," said he, grinning again. "Queequeg here wouldn't harm a hair of your head."

"Stop your grinning," shouted I, "and why didn't you tell me that that infernal harpooneer was a cannibal?"

"I thought ye know'd it;—didn't I tell ye, he was a peddlin' heads around town?—but turn flukes again and go to sleep, Queequeg, look here—you sabbee me, I sabbee you—this man sleepe you—you sabbee?"—

"Me sabbee plenty"—grunted Queequeg, puffing away at his pipe and sitting up in bed.

"You gettee in," he added, motioning to me with his tomahawk, and throwing the clothes to one side. He really did this in not only a civil but a really kind and charitable way. I stood looking at

[43]

him a moment. For all his tattooings he was on the whole a clean, comely looking cannibal. What's all this fuss I have been making about, thought I to myself—the man's a human being just as I am: he has just as much reason to fear me, as I have to be afraid of him. Better sleep with a sober cannibal than a drunken Christian.

"Landlord," said I, "tell him to stash his tomahawk there, or pipe, or whatever you call it; tell him to stop smoking, in short, and I will turn in with him. But I don't fancy having a man smoking in bed with me. It's dangerous. Besides, I aint insured."

This being told to Queequeg, he at once complied, and again politely motioned me to get into bed—rolling over to one side as much as to say—I wont touch a leg of ye.

"Good night, landlord," said I, "you may go."

I turned in, and never slept better in my life.

THE COUNTERPANE

Upon waking next morning about daylight, I found Queequeg's arm thrown over me in the most loving and affectionate manner. You had almost thought I had been his wife. The counterpane was of patchwork, full of odd little parti-colored squares and triangles; and this arm of his tattooed all over with an interminable Cretan labyrinth of a figure, no two parts of which were of one precise shade—owing I suppose to his keeping his arm at sea unmethodically in sun and shade, his shirt sleeves irregularly rolled up at various times—this same arm of his, I say, looked for all the world like a strip of that same patchwork quilt. Indeed, partly lying on it as the arm did when I first awoke, I could hardly tell it from the quilt, they so blended their hues together; and it was only by the sense of weight and pressure that I could tell that Queequeg was hugging me.

My sensations were strange. Let me try to explain them. When I was a child, I well remember a somewhat similar circumstance that befell me; whether it was a reality or a dream, I never could entirely settle. The circumstance was this. I had been cutting up some caper or other—I think it was trying to crawl up the chimney, as I had seen a little sweep do a few days previous; and my stepmother who, somehow or other, was all the time whipping me, or sending me to bed supperless,—my mother dragged me by the legs out of the chimney and packed me off to bed, though it was only two o'clock in the afternoon of the 21st June, the longest day in the year in our hemisphere. I felt dreadfully. But there was no help for it, so up stairs I went to my little room in the third floor, undressed myself as slowly as possible so as to kill time, and with a bitter sigh got between the sheets.

I lay there dismally calculating that sixteen entire hours must elapse before I could hope for a resurrection. Sixteen hours in bed! the small of my back ached to think of it. And it was so light too; the sun shining in at the window, and a great rattling of coaches in the streets, and the sound of gay voices all over the house. I felt worse and worse—at last I got up, dressed, and softly going down in my stockinged feet, sought out my stepmother, and suddenly threw myself at her feet, beseeching her as a particular favor to give me a good slippering for my misbehavior; anything indeed but condemning me to lie abed such an unendurable length of time. But she was the best and most conscientious of stepmothers, and back I had to go to my room. For several hours I lay there broad awake, feeling a great deal worse than I have ever done since, even from the greatest subsequent misfortunes. At last I must have fallen into a troubled nightmare of a doze; and slowly waking from it—half steeped in dreams— I opened my eyes, and the before sunlit room was now wrapped in outer darkness. Instantly I felt a shock running through all my frame; nothing was to be seen, and nothing was to be heard; but a supernatural hand seemed placed in mine. My arm hung over the counterpane, and the nameless, unimaginable, silent form or phantom, to which the hand belonged, seemed closely seated by my bed-side. For what seemed ages piled on ages, I lay there, frozen with the most awful fears, not daring to drag away my hand; yet ever thinking that if I could but stir it one single inch, the horrid spell would be broken. I knew not how this consciousness at last glided away from me; but waking in the morning, I shudderingly remembered it all, and for days and weeks and months afterwards I lost myself in confounding attempts to explain the mystery. Nay, to this very hour, I often puzzle myself with it.

Now, take away the awful fear, and my sensations at feeling the supernatural hand in mine were very similar, in their strangeness, to those which I experienced on waking up and seeing Queequeg's pagan arm thrown round me. But at length all the past night's events soberly recurred, one by one, in fixed reality, and then I lay only alive to the comical predicament. For though I tried to move his arm— unlock his bridegroom clasp—yet, sleeping as he was, he still hugged me tightly, as though naught but death should part us twain. I now strove to rouse him—"Queequeg!"—but his only answer was a snore. I then rolled over, my neck feeling as if it were in a horse-collar; and suddenly felt a slight scratch. Throwing aside the counterpane, there lay the tomahawk sleeping by the savage's side, as if it were a hatchet-faced baby. A pretty pickle, truly, thought I; abed here in a strange house in the broad day, with a cannibal and a tomahawk! "Queequeg!—in the name of goodness, Queequeg, wake!"

At length, by dint of much wriggling, and loud and incessant expostulations upon the unbecomingness of his hugging a fellow male in that matrimonial sort of style, I succeeded in extracting a grunt; and presently, he drew back his arm, shook himself all over like a Newfoundland dog just from the water, and sat up in bed, stiff as a pike-staff, looking at me, and rubbing his eyes as if he did not altogether remember how I came to be there, though a dim consciousness of knowing something about me seemed slowly dawning over him. Meanwhile, I lay quietly eyeing him, having no serious misgivings now, and bent upon narrowly observing so curious a creature. When, at last, his mind seemed made up touching the character of his bedfellow, and he became, as it were, reconciled to the fact; he jumped out upon the floor, and by certain signs and sounds gave me to understand that, if it pleased me, he would dress first and then leave me to dress afterwards, leaving the whole apartment to myself. Thinks I, Queequeg, under the circumstances, this is a very civilized overture; but, the truth is, these savages have an innate sense of delicacy, say what you will; it is marvellous how essentially polite they are. I pay this particular compliment to Queequeg, because he treated me with so much civility and consideration, while I was guilty of great rudeness; staring at him from the bed, and watching all his toilette motions; for the time my curiosity getting the better of my breeding. Nevertheless, a man like Queequeg you don't see every day, he and his ways were well worth unusual regarding.

He commenced dressing at top by donning his beaver hat, a very tall one, by the by, and then—still minus his trowsers—he hunted up his boots. What under the heavens he did it for, I cannot tell, but his next movement was to crush himself—boots in hand, and hat on—under the bed; when, from sundry violent gaspings and strainings, I inferred he was hard at work booting himself; though by no law of propriety that I ever heard of, is any man required to be private when putting on his boots. But Queequeg, do you see, was a creature in the transition stage—neither caterpillar nor butterfly. He was just enough civilized to show off his outlandishness in the strangest possible manners. His education was not yet completed. He was an undergraduate. If he had not been a small degree civilized, he very probably would not have troubled himself with boots at all; but then, if he had not been still a savage, he never would have dreamt of getting under the bed to put them on. At last, he emerged with his hat very much dented and crushed down over his eyes, and began creaking and limping about the room, as if, not being much accustomed to boots, his pair of damp, wrinkled cowhide ones—probably not made to order either—rather pinched and tormented him at the first go off of a bitter cold morning.

Seeing, now, that there were no curtains to the window, and that the street being very narrow, the house opposite commanded a plain view into the room, and observing more and more the indecorous figure that Queequeg made, staving about with little else but his hat and boots on; I begged him as well as I could, to accelerate his toilet somewhat, and particularly to get into his pantaloons as soon as possible. He complied, and then proceeded to wash himself. At that time in the morning any Christian would have washed his face; but Queequeg, to my amazement, contented himself with restricting his ablutions to his chest, arms, and hands. He then donned his waistcoat, and taking up a piece of hard soap on the wash-stand centre table, dipped it into water and commenced lathering his face. I was watching to see where he kept his razor, when lo and behold, he takes the harpoon from the bed corner, slips out the long wooden stock, unsheathes the head, whets it a little on his boot, and striding up to the bit of mirror against the wall, begins a vigorous scraping, or rather harpooning of his cheeks. Thinks I, Queequeg, this is using Rogers's best cutlery with a vengeance. Afterwards I wondered the less at this operation when I came to know of what fine steel the head of a harpoon is made, and how exceedingly sharp the long straight edges are always kept.

The rest of his toilet was soon achieved, and he proudly marched out of the room, wrapped up in his great pilot monkey jacket, and sporting his harpoon like a marshal's baton.

BREAKFAST

I quickley followed suit, and descending into the bar-room accosted the grinning landlord very pleasantly. I cherished no malice towards him, though he had been skylarking with me not a little in the matter of my bedfellow.

However, a good laugh is a mighty good thing, and rather too scarce a good thing; the more's the pity. So, if any one man, in his own proper person, afford stuff for a good joke to anybody, let him not be backward, but let him cheerfully allow himself to spend and to be spent in that way. And the man that has anything bountifully laughable about him, be sure there is more in that man than you perhaps think for.

The bar-room was now full of the boarders who had been dropping in the night previous, and whom I had not as yet had a good look at. They were nearly all whalemen; chief mates, and second mates, and third mates, and sea carpenters, and sea coopers, and sea blacksmiths, and harpooneers, and ship keepers; a brown and brawny company, with bosky beards; an unshorn, shaggy set, all wearing monkey jackets for morning gowns.

You could pretty plainly tell how long each one had been ashore. This young fellow's healthy cheek is like a sun-toasted pear in hue, and would seem to smell almost as musky; he cannot have been three days landed from his Indian voyage. That man next him looks a few shades lighter; you might say a touch of satin wood is in him. In the complexion of a third still lingers a tropic tawn, but slightly bleached withal; *he* doubtless has tarried whole weeks ashore. But who could show a cheek like Queequeg? which, barred with various tints, seemed like the Andes' western slope, to show forth in one array, contrasting climates, zone by zone.

"Grub, ho!" now cried the landlord, flinging open a door, and in we went to breakfast.

They say that men who have seen the world, thereby become quite at ease in manner, quite self-possessed in company. Not always, though: Ledyard, the great New England traveller, and Mungo Park, the Scotch one; of all men, they possessed the least assurance in the parlor. But perhaps the mere crossing of Siberia in a sledge drawn by dogs as Ledyard did, or the taking a long solitary walk on an empty stomach, in the negro heart of Africa, which was the sum of poor Mungo's performances—this kind of travel, I say, may not be the very best mode of attaining a high social polish. Still, for the most part, that sort of thing is to be had anywhere.

These reflections just here are occasioned by the circumstance that after we were all seated at the table, and I was preparing to hear some good stories about whaling; to my no small surprise, nearly every man maintained a profound silence. And not only that, but they looked embarrassed. Yes, here were a set of sea-dogs, many of whom without the slightest bashfulness had boarded great whales on the high seas—entire strangers to them—and duelled them dead without winking; and yet, here they sat at a social breakfast table—all of the same calling, all of kindred tastes—looking round as sheepishly at each other as though they had never been out of sight of some sheepfold among the Green Mountains. A curious sight; these bashful bears, these timid warrior whalemen!

But as for Queequeg—why, Queequeg sat there among them—at the head of the table, too, it so chanced; as cool as an icicle. To be sure I cannot say much for his breeding. His greatest admirer could not have cordially justified his bringing his harpoon into breakfast with him, and using it there without ceremony; reaching over the table with it, to the imminent jeopardy of many heads, and grappling the beefsteaks towards him. But *that* was certainly very coolly done by him, and every one knows that in most people's estimation, to do anything coolly is to do it genteelly.

We will not speak of all Queequeg's peculiarities here; how he eschewed coffee and hot rolls, and applied his undivided attention to beefsteaks, done rare. Enough, that when breakfast was over he withdrew like the rest into the public room, lighted his tomahawk-pipe, and was sitting there quietly digesting and smoking with his inseparable hat on, when I sallied out for a stroll.

THE STREET

If I had been astonished at first catching a glimpse of so outlandish an individual as Queequeg circulating among the polite society of a civilized town, that astonishment soon departed upon taking my first daylight stroll through the streets of New Bedford.

In thoroughfares nigh the docks, any considerable seaport will frequently offer to view the queerest looking nondescripts from foreign parts. Even in Broadway and Chestnut streets, Mediterranean mariners will sometimes jostle the affrighted ladies. Regent street is not unknown to Lascars and Malays; and at Bombay, in the Apollo Green, live Yankees have often scared the natives. But New Bedford beats all Water street and Wapping. In these last-mentioned haunts you see only sailors; but in New Bedford, actual cannibals stand chatting at street corners; savages outright; many of whom yet carry on their bones unholy flesh. It makes a stranger stare.

But, besides the Feegeeans, Tongatabooans, Erro-manggoans, Pannangians, and Brighggians, and, be-sides the wild specimens of the whaling-craft which unheeded reel about the streets, you will see other sights still more curious, certainly more comical. There weekly arrive in this town scores of green Vermonters and New Hampshire men, all athirst for gain and glory in the fishery. They are mostly young, of stalwart frames; fellows who have felled forests, and now seek to drop the axe and snatch the whale-lance. Many are as green as the Green Mountains whence they come. In some things you would think them but a few hours old. Look there! that chap strutting round the corner. He wears a beaver hat and swallow-tailed coat, girdled with a sailor-belt and sheath-knife. Here comes another with a sou'-wester and a bombazine cloak.

No town-bred dandy will compare with a country-bred one—I mean a downright bumpkin dandy—a fellow that, in the dog-days, will mow his two acres in buckskin gloves for fear of tanning his hands. Now when a country dandy like this takes it into his head to make a distinguished reputation, and joins the great whale-fishery, you should see the comical things he does upon reaching the seaport. In be-speaking his sea-outfit, he orders bell-buttons to his waistcoats; straps to his canvas trowsers. Ah, poor

Hay-Seed! how bitterly will burst those straps in the first howling gale, when thou art driven, straps, buttons, and all, down the throat of the tempest.

But think not that this famous town has only harpooneers, cannibals, and bumpkins to show her visitors. Not at all. Still New Bedford is a queer place. Had it not been for us whalemen, that tract of land would this day perhaps have been in as howling condition as the coast of Labrador. As it is, parts of her back country are enough to frighten one, they look so bony. The town itself is perhaps the dearest place to live in, in all New England. It is a land of oil, true enough: but not like Canaan, a land, also, of corn and wine. The streets do not run with milk; nor in the spring-time do they pave them with fresh eggs. Yet, in spite of this, nowhere in all America will you find more patrician-like houses, parks and gardens more opulent, than in New Bedford. Whence came they? how planted upon this once scraggy scoria of a country?

Go and gaze upon the iron emblematical harpoons round yonder lofty mansion, and your question will be answered. Yes; all these brave houses and flowery gardens came from the Atlantic, Pacific, and Indian oceans. One and all, they were harpooned and dragged up hither from the bottom of the sea. Can Herr Alexander perform a feat like that?

In New Bedford, fathers, they say, give whales for dowers to their daughters, and portion off their nieces with a few porpoises a-piece. You must go to New Bedford to see a brilliant wedding; for, they say, they have reservoirs of oil in every house, and every night recklessly burn their lengths in spermaceti candles.

In summer time, the town is sweet to see; full of fine maples— long avenues of green and gold. And in August, high in air, the beautiful and bountiful horse-chestnuts, candelabra-wise, proffer the passer-by their tapering upright cones of congregated blossoms. So omnipotent is art; which in many a district of New Bedford has superinduced bright terraces of flowers upon the barren refuse rocks thrown aside at creation's final day.

And the women of New Bedford, they bloom like their own red roses. But roses only bloom in summer; whereas the fine carnation of their cheeks is perennial as sunlight in the seventh heavens. Elsewhere match that bloom of theirs, ye cannot, save in Salem, where they tell me the young girls breathe such musk, their sailor sweethearts smell them miles off shore, as though they were drawing nigh the odorous Moluccas instead of the Puritanic sands.

THE CHAPEL

In this same New Bedford there stands a Whaleman's Chapel, and few are the moody fishermen, shortly bound for the Indian Ocean or Pacific, who fail to make a Sunday visit to the spot. I am sure that I did not.

Returning from my first morning stroll, I again sallied out upon this special errand. The sky had changed from clear, sunny cold, to driving sleet and mist. Wrapping myself in my shaggy jacket of the cloth called bearskin, I fought my way against the stubborn storm. Entering, I found a small scattered congregation of sailors, and sailors' wives and widows. A muffled silence reigned, only broken at times by the shrieks of the storm. Each silent worshipper seemed purposely sitting apart from the other, as if each silent grief were insular and incommunicable. The chaplain had not yet arrived; and there these silent islands of men and women sat steadfastly eyeing several marble tablets, with black borders, masoned into the wall on either side the pulpit. Three of them ran something like the following, but I do not pretend to quote:—

SACRED

To the Memory

OF

JOHN TALBOT,

Who, at the age of eighteen, was lost overboard,
Near the Isle of Desolation, off Patagonia,
November 1st, 1836.

THIS TABLET
Is erected to his Memory
BY HIS SISTER.

SACRED

𝔗𝔬 𝔱𝔥𝔢 𝔐𝔢𝔪𝔬𝔯𝔶

O F

ROBERT LONG, WILLIS ELLERY,
NATHAN COLEMAN, WALTER CANNY,
SETH MACY, AND SAMUEL GLEIG,

Forming one of the boats' crews

O F

THE SHIP ELIZA,

Who were towed out of sight by a Whale,
On the Off-shore Ground in the

PACIFIC,
December 31st, 1839.

THIS MARBLE
Is here placed by their surviving

Shipmates.

SACRED

𝔗𝔬 𝔱𝔥𝔢 𝔐𝔢𝔪𝔬𝔯𝔶

O F

The late
CAPTAIN EZEKIEL HARDY,

Who in the bows of his boat was killed by a
Sperm Whale on the coast of Japan,
August 3d, 1833.

THIS TABLET
Is erected to his Memory

B Y

HIS WIDOW.

Shaking off the sleet from my ice-glazed hat and
jacket, I seated myself near the door, and turning
sideways was surprised to see Queequeg near me.
Affected by the solemnity of the scene, there was a

wondering gaze of incredulous curiosity in his countenance. This savage was the only person present who seemed to notice my entrance; because he was the only one who could not read, and, therefore, was not reading those frigid inscriptions on the wall. Whether any of the relatives of the seamen whose names appeared there were now among the congregation, I knew not; but so many are the unrecorded accidents in the fishery, and so plainly did several women present wear the countenance if not the trappings of some unceasing grief, that I feel sure that here before me were assembled those, in whose unhealing hearts the sight of those bleak tablets sympathetically caused the old wounds to bleed afresh.

Oh! ye whose dead lie buried beneath the green grass; who standing among flowers can say—here, *here* lies my beloved; ye know not the desolation that broods in bosoms like these. What bitter blanks in those black-bordered marbles which cover no ashes! What despair in those immovable inscriptions! What deadly voids and unbidden infidelities in the lines that seem to gnaw upon all Faith, and refuse resurrections to the beings who have placelessly perished without a grave. As well might those tablets stand in the cave of Elephanta as here.

In what census of living creatures, the dead of mankind are included; why it is that a universal proverb says of them, that they tell no tales, though

containing more secrets than the Goodwin Sands;
how it is that to his name who yesterday departed
for the other world, we prefix so significant and
infidel a word, and yet do not thus entitle him, if he
but embarks for the remotest Indies of this living
earth; why the Life Insurance Companies pay death-
forfeitures upon immortals; in what eternal, unstir-
ring paralysis, and deadly, hopeless trance, yet lies
antique Adam who died sixty round centuries ago;
how it is that we still refuse to be comforted for
those who we nevertheless maintain are dwelling in
unspeakable bliss; why all the living so strive to hush
all the dead; wherefore but the rumor of a knocking
in a tomb will terrify a whole city. All these things
are not without their meanings.

But Faith, like a jackal, feeds among the tombs,
and even from these dead doubts she gathers her
most vital hope.

It needs scarcely to be told, with what feelings, on
the eve of a Nantucket voyage, I regarded those marble tablets, and by the murky light of that darkened,
doleful day read the fate of the whalemen who had
gone before me. Yes, Ishmael, the same fate may be
thine. But somehow I grew merry again. Delightful
inducements to embark, fine chance for promotion,
it seems—aye, a stove boat will make me an immortal by brevet. Yes, there is death in this business of
whaling—a speechlessly quick chaotic bundling of
a man into Eternity. But what then? Methinks we

have hugely mistaken this matter of Life and Death. Methinks that what they call my shadow here on earth is my true substance. Methinks that in looking at things spiritual, we are too much like oysters observing the sun through the water, and thinking that thick water the thinnest of air. Methinks my body is but the lees of my better being. In fact take my body who will, take it I say, it is not me. And therefore three cheers for Nantucket; and come a stove boat and stove body when they will, for stave my soul, Jove himself cannot.

NANTUCKET

Nothing more happened on the passage worthy the mentioning; so, after a fine run, we safely arrived in Nantucket.

Nantucket! Take out your map and look at it. See what a real corner of the world it occupies; how it stands there, away off shore, more lonely than the Eddystone lighthouse. Look at it—a mere hillock, and elbow of sand; all beach, without a background. There is more sand there than you would use in twenty years as a substitute for blotting paper. Some gamesome wights will tell you that they have to plant weeds there, they don't grow naturally; that they import Canada thistles; that they have to send beyond seas for a spile to stop a leak in an oil cask;

that pieces of wood in Nantucket are carried about like bits of the true cross in Rome; that people there plant toadstools before their houses, to get under the shade in summer time; that one blade of grass makes an oasis, three blades in a day's walk a prairie; that they wear quicksand shoes, something like Laplander snow-shoes; that they are so shut up, belted about, every way enclosed, surrounded, and made an utter island of by the ocean, that to their very chairs and tables small clams will sometimes be found adhering, as to the backs of sea turtles. But these extravaganzas only show that Nantucket is no Illinois.

Look now at the wondrous traditional story of how this island was settled by the red-men. Thus goes the legend. In olden times an eagle swooped down upon the New England coast, and carried off an infant Indian in his talons. With loud lament the parents saw their child borne out of sight over the wide waters. They resolved to follow in the same direction. Setting out in their canoes, after a perilous passage they discovered the island, and there they found an empty ivory casket,—the poor little Indian's skeleton.

What wonder, then, that these Nantucketers, born on a beach, should take to the sea for a livelihood! They first caught crabs and quohogs in the sand; grown bolder, they waded out with nets for mackerel; more experienced, they pushed off in boats and captured cod; and at last, launching a navy of great ships on the sea, explored this watery world; put an incessant belt of circumnavigations round it; peeped in at Behring's Straits; and in all seasons and all oceans declared everlasting war with the mightiest animated mass that has survived the flood; most monstrous and most mountainous! That Himmalehan, salt-sea Mastodon, clothed with such portentousness of unconscious power, that his very panics are more to be dreaded than his most fearless and malicious assaults!

And thus have these naked Nantucketers, these sea hermits, issuing from their ant-hill in the sea, over-run and conquered the watery world like so many Alexanders; parcelling out among them the Atlantic, Pacific, and Indian oceans, as the three pirate powers did Poland. Let America add Mexico to Texas, and pile Cuba upon Canada; let the English overswarm all India, and hang out their blazing banner from the sun; two thirds of this terraqueous globe are the Nantucketer's. For the sea is his; he owns it, as Emperors own empires; other seamen having but a right of way through it. Merchant ships are but extension bridges; armed ones but floating forts; even pirates and privateers, though following the sea is highwaymen the road, they but plunder other ship, other fragments of the land like themselves, without seeking to draw their living from the bottomless deep itself. The Nantucketer, he alone resides and riots on the sea; he alone, in Bible language, goes down to it in ships; to and fro ploughing it as his own special plantation. *There* is his home; *there* lies his business, which a Noah's flood would not interrupt, though it overwhelmed all the millions in China. He lives on the sea, as prairie cocks in the prairie; he hides among the waves, he climbs them as chamois hunters climb the Alps. For years he knows not the land; so that when he comes to it at last, it smells like another world, more strangely than the moon would to an Earthsman. With the landless gull, that at sunset folds her wings and is rocked to sleep between billows; so at nightfall, the Nantucketer, out of sight of land, furls his sails, and lays him to his rest, while under his very pillow rush herds of walruses and whales.

Marsh Rosemary

[S A R A H   O R N E   J E W E T T]

I

One hot afternoon in August, a single moving figure might have been seen following a straight road that crossed the salt marshes of Walpole. Everybody else had either stayed at home or crept into such shade as could be found near at hand. The thermometer marked at least ninety degrees. There was hardly a fishing-boat to be seen on the glistening sea, only far away on the hazy horizon two or three coasting schooners looked like ghostly Flying Dutchmen, becalmed for once and motionless.

Ashore, the flaring light of the sun brought out the fine, clear colors of the level landscape. The marsh grasses were a more vivid green than usual, the brown tops of those that were beginning to go to seed looked almost red, and the soil at the edges of the tide inlets seemed to be melting into a black, pitchy substance like the dark pigments on a painter's palette. Where the land was higher the hot air flickered above it dizzily. This was not an afternoon that one would naturally choose for a long walk, yet Mr. Jerry Lane stepped briskly forward, and appeared to have more than usual energy. His big boots trod down the soft carpet of pussy-clover that bordered the dusty, whitish road. He struck at the stationary procession of thistles with a little stick as he went by. Flight after flight of yellow butterflies fluttered up as he passed, and then wavered down again to their thistle flowers, while on the shiny cambric back of Jerry's Sunday waistcoat basked at least eight large green-headed flies in complete security.

It was difficult to decide why the Sunday waistcoat should have been put on that Saturday afternoon. Jerry had not thought it important to wear his best boots or best trousers, and had left his coat at home altogether. He smiled as he walked along, and once when he took off his hat, as a light breeze came that way, he waved it triumphantly before he put it on again. Evidently this was no common errand that led him due west, and made him forget the hot weather, and caused him to shade his eyes with his hand, as he looked eagerly at a clump of trees and the chimney of a small house a littleway beyond the boundary of the marshes, where the higher ground began.

Miss Ann Floyd sat by her favorite window, sewing, twitching her thread less decidedly than usual, and casting a wistful glance now and then down the road, or at the bees in her gay little garden outside. There was a grim expression overshadowing her firmly-set, angular face, and the frown that always appeared on her forehead when she sewed or read the newspaper was deeper and straighter than usual. She did not look as if she were conscious of the heat, though she had dressed herself in an old-fashioned skirt of sprigged lawn and a loose jacket of thin white dimity with out-of-date flowing sleeves. Her sandy hair was smoothly brushed; one lock betrayed a slight crinkle at its edge, but it owed nothing to any encouragement of Nancy Floyd's. A hard, honest, kindly face this was, of a woman whom everybody trusted, who might be expected to give of whatever she had to give, good measure, pressed down and running over. She was a lonely soul; she had no near relatives in the world. It seemed always as if nature had been mistaken in not planting her somewhere in a large and busy household.

The little square room, kitchen in winter and sitting-room in summer, was as clean and bare and thrifty as one would expect the dwelling-place of such a woman to be. She sat in a straight-backed, splint-bottomed kitchen chair, and always put back her spool with a click on the very same spot on the window-sill. You would think she had done with youth and with love affairs, yet you might as well expect the ancient cherry-tree in the corner of her yard to cease adventuring its white blossoms when the May sun shone! No woman in Walpole had more bravely and patiently borne the burden of loneliness and lack of love. Even now her outward behavior gave no hint of the new excitement and delight that filled her heart.

"Land sakes alive!" she says to herself presently, "there comes Jerry Lane. I expect, if he sees me set-tin' to the winder, he'll come in an' dawdle round till suppertime!" But good Nancy Floyd smooths her hair hastily as she rises and drops her work, and steps back toward the middle of the room, watching the gate anxiously all the time. Now, Jerry, with a crestfallen look at the vacant window, makes believe that he is going by, and takes a loitering step or two onward, and then stops short; with a somewhat sheepish smile he leans over the neat picket fence and examines the blue and white and pink larkspur that covers most of the space in the little garden. He takes off his hat again to cool his forehead, and replaces it, without a grand gesture this time, and looks again at the window hopefully. There is a pause. The woman knows that the man is sure she is there; a little blush colors her thin cheeks as she comes boldly to the wide-open front door.

"What do you think of this kind of weather?" asks Jerry Lane complacently, as he leans over the fence, and surrounds himself with an air of self-sacrifice.

"I call it hot," responds the Juliet from her balcony, with deliberate assurance, "but the corn needs sun, everybody says. I should n't have wanted to toil up from the shore under such a glare, if I had been you. Better come in and set awhile, and cool off," she added, without any apparent enthusiasm. Jerry was sure to come, anyway. She would rather make the suggestion than have him.

Mr. Lane sauntered in, and seated himself opposite his hostess, beside the other small window, and watched her admiringly as she took up her sewing and worked at it with great spirit and purpose. He clasped his hands together and leaned forward a little. The shaded kitchen was very comfortable, after the glaring light outside, and the clean orderliness of the few chairs, and the braided rugs, and the table under the clock, with some larkspur and asparagus in a china vase for decoration, seemed to please him unexpectedly. "Now just see what ways you women folks have of fixing things up smart!" he ventured gallantly.

Nancy's countenance did not forbid further compliment; she looked at the flowers herself, quickly, and explained that she had gathered them a while ago to send to the minister's sister, who kept house for him. "I saw him going by, and expected he'd be back this same road. Mis' Elton's be'n havin' another o' her dyin' spells this noon, and the deacon went by after him hot foot. I'd souse her well with stone-cold water. She never sent for me to set up with her; she knows better. Poor man, 't was likely he was right into the middle of to-morrow's sermon. 'T ain't considerate of the deacon, and when he knows he's got a fool for a wife, he need n't go round persuading other folks she's so suffering as she makes out. They ain't got no larkspur this year to the parsonage, and I was going to let the minister take this over to Amandy; but I see his wagon over on the other road, going towards the village, about an hour after he went by here."

It seemed to be a relief to tell somebody all these things after such a season of forced repression, and Jerry listened with gratifying interest. "How you do see through folks!" he exclaimed in a mild voice. Jerry could be very soft spoken if he thought best. "Mis' Elton's a die-away lookin' creatur'. I heard of her saying last Sunday, comin' out o' meetin', that she made an effort to git there once more, but she expected 't would be the last time. Looks at if she eat well, don't she?" he concluded in a meditative tone.

"Eat!" exclaimed the hostess, with snapping eyes. "There ain't no woman in town, sick or well, can lay aside the food that she does. 'T ain't to the table afore folks, but she goes seeking round in the cupboards half a dozen times a day. An' I've heard her remark 't was the last time she ever expected to visit the sanctuary as much as a dozen times within five years."

"Some places I've sailed to they'd have hit her over the head with a club long ago," said Jerry, with an utter lack of sympathy that was startling. "Well, I must be gettin' back again. Talkin' of eatin' makes us think o' supper-time. Must be past five, ain't it? I thought I'd just step up to see if there wa'n't anything I could lend a hand about, this hot day."

Sensible Ann Floyd folded her hands over her sewing, as it lay in her lap, and looked straight before her without seeing the pleading face of the guest. This moment was a great crisis in her life. She was conscious of it, and knew well enough that upon her next words would depend the course of future events. The man who waited to hear what she had to say was indeed many years younger than she, was shiftless and vacillating. He had drifted to Walpole from nobody knew where and possessed many qualities which she had openly rebuked and despised in other men. True enough, he was good-looking, but that did not atone for the lacks of his character and reputation. Yet she knew herself to be the better man of the two, and since she had surmounted many obstacles already she was confident that, with a push here and a pull there to steady him, she could keep him in good trim. The winters were so long and lonely; her life was in many ways hungry and desolate in spite of its thrift and conformity. She had laughed scornfully when he stopped, one day in the spring, and offered to help her weed her garden; she had even joked with one of the neighbors about it. Jerry had been growing more and more friendly and pleasant ever since. His ease-loving, careless nature was like a comfortable cushion for hers, with its angles, its melancholy anticipations and self-questionings. But Jerry liked her, and if she liked him and married him, and took him home, it was nobody's business; and in that moment of surrender to Jerry's cause she arrayed herself at his right hand against the rest of the world, ready for warfare with any and all of its opinions.

She was suddenly aware of the sunburnt face and light, curling hair of her undeclared lover, at the other end of the painted table with its folded leaf. She smiled at him vacantly across the larkspur; then she gave a little start, and was afraid that her thoughts had wandered longer than was seemly. The kitchen clock was ticking faster than usual, as if it were trying to attract attention.

"I guess I'll be getting home," repeated the visitor ruefully, and rose from his chair, but hesitated again at an unfamiliar expression upon his companion's face.

"I don't know as I've got anything extra for supper, but you stop," she said, "an' take what there is. I would n't go back across them marshes right in this heat."

Jerry Lane had a lively sense of humor, and a queer feeling of merriment stole over him now, as he watched the mistress of the house. She had risen, too; she looked so simple and so frankly sentimental, there was such an incongruous coyness added to her usually straightforward, angular appearance, that his instinctive laughter nearly got the better of him, and might have lost him the prize for which he had been waiting these many months. But Jerry behaved like a man: he stepped forward and kissed Ann Floyd; he held her fast with one arm as he stood beside her, and kissed her again and again. She was a dear good woman. She had a fresh young heart, in spite of the straight wrinkle in her forehead and her work-worn hands. She had waited all her days for this joy of having a lover.

II

Even Mrs. Elton revived for a day or two under the tonic of such a piece of news. That was what Jerry Lane had hung round for all summer, everybody knew at last. Now he would strike work and live at his ease, the men grumbled to each other; but all the women of Walpole deplored most the weakness and foolishness of the elderly bride. Ann Floyd was comfortably off, and had something laid by for a rainy day; she would have done vastly better to deny herself such an expensive and utterly worthless luxury as the kind of husband Jerry Lane would make. He had idled away his life. He earned a little money now and then in seafaring pursuits, but was too lazy, in the shore parlance, to tend lobster-pots. What was energetic Ann Floyd going to do with him? She was always at work, always equal to emergencies, and entirely opposed to dullness and idleness and even placidity. She often avowed scornfully that she liked people who had some snap to them, and now she had chosen for a husband the laziest man in Walpole. "Dear sakes," one woman said to another, as they heard the news, "there's no fool like an old fool!"

The days went quickly by, while Miss Ann made her plain wedding clothes. If people expected her to put on airs of youth they were disappointed. Her wedding bonnet was the same sort of bonnet she had worn for a dozen years, and one disappointed critic deplored the fact that she had spruced up so little, and kept on dressing old enough to look like Jerry Lane's mother. As her acquaintances met her they looked at her with close scrutiny, expecting to see some outward trace of such a silly, uncharacteristic departure from good sense and discretion. But Miss Floyd, while she was still Miss Floyd, displayed no silliness and behaved with dignity, while on the Sunday after a quiet marriage at the parsonage she and Jerry Lane walked up the side aisle together to their pew, the picture of middle-aged sobriety and respectability. Their fellow-parishioners, having recovered from their first astonishment and amusement, settled down to the belief that the newly married pair understood their own business best and that if anybody could make the best of Jerry and get any work out of him, it was his capable wife.

"And if she undertakes to drive him too hard he can slip off to sea, and they'll be rid of each other," commented one of Jerry's 'longshore companions, as if it were only reasonable that some refuge should be afforded to those who make mistakes in matrimony.

There did not seem to be any mistake at first, or for a good many months afterward. The husband liked the comfort that came from such good housekeeping, and enjoyed a deep sense of having made a good anchorage in a well-sheltered harbor, after many years of thriftless improvidence and drifting to and fro. There were some hindrances to perfect happiness: he had to forego long seasons of gossip with his particular friends, and the outdoor work which was expected of him, though by no means heavy for a person of his strength, fettered his freedom not a little. To chop wood, and take care of a cow, and bring a pail of water now and then, did not weary him so much as it made him practically understand the truth of weakly Sister Elton's remark, that life was a constant chore. And when poor Jerry, for lack of other interest, fancied that his health was giving way mysteriously, and brought home a bottle of strong liquor to be used in case of sickness, and placed it conveniently in the shed, Mrs.

Lane locked it up in the small chimney cupboard where she kept her camphor bottle and her opodeldoc and the other family medicines. She was not harsh with her husband. She cherished him tenderly, and worked diligently at her trade of tailoress, singing her hymns gayly in summer weather; for she never had been so happy as now, when there was somebody to please beside herself, to cook for and sew for, and to live with and love. But Jerry complained more and more in his inmost heart that his wife expected too much of him. Presently he resumed an old habit of resorting to the least respected of the two country stores of that neighborhood, and sat in the row of loafers on the outer steps. "Sakes alive," said a shrewd observer one day, "the fools set there and talk and talk about what they went through when they follered the sea, and when the women-folks comes tradin' they are obleeged to climb right over 'em."

Things grew worse and worse, until one day Jerry Lane came home a little late to dinner, and found his wife unusually grim-faced and impatient. He took his seat with an amiable smile, and showed in every way a fine determination not to lose his temper because somebody else had. It was one of the days when he looked almost boyish and entirely irresponsible. His hair was bright and curly from the dampness of the east wind, and his wife was forced to remember how, in the days of their courtship, she used to wish that she could pull one of the curling locks straight, for the pleasure of seeing it fly back. Nancy felt old and tired, and was hurt in her very soul by the contrast between herself and her husband. "No wonder I am aging, having to lug everything on my shoulders," she thought. Jerry had forgotten to do whatever she had asked him for a day or two. He had started out that morning to go lobstering, but returned from the direction of the village.

"Nancy," he said pleasantly, after he had begun his dinner, a silent and solitary meal, while his wife stitched busily by the window, and refused to look at him. "Nancy, I've been thinking a good deal about a project."

"I hope it ain't going to cost so much and bring in so little as your other notions have, then," she responded quickly; though somehow a memory of the hot day when Jerry came and stood outside the fence, and kissed her when it was settled he should stay to supper,—a memory of that day would keep fading and brightening in her mind.

"Yes," said Jerry humbly, "I ain't done right, Nancy. I ain't done my part for our livin'. I've let it sag right on to you, most ever since we was married. There was that spell when I was kind of weakly, and had a pain acrost me. I tell you what it is: I never was good for nothin' ashore, but now I've got my strength up I'm going to show ye what I can do.

I'm promised to ship with Cap'n Low's brother, Skipper Nathan, that sails out o' Eastport in the coasting trade, lumber and so on. I shall get good wages and you shall keep the whole on 't 'cept what I need for clothes."

"You need n't be so plaintive," said Ann in a sharp voice. "You can go if you want to. I have always been able to take care of myself, but when it comes to maintainin' two 't ain't so easy. When be you goin'?"

"I expected you would be distressed," mourned Jerry, his face falling at this outbreak. "Nancy, you need n't be so quick. 'Tain't as if I had n't always set consid'able by ye, if I be wuthless."

Nancy's eyes flashed fire as she turned hastily away. Hardly knowing where she went, she passed though the open doorway, and crossed the clean green turf of the narrow side yard, and leaned over the garden fence. The young cabbages and cucumbers were nearly buried in weeds, and the currant bushes were fast being turned into skeletons by the ravaging worms. Jerry had forgotten to sprinkle them with hellebore, after all, though she had put the watering-pot into his very hand the evening before. She did not like to have the whole town laugh at her for hiring a man to do his work; she was busy from early morning until late night, but she could not do everything herself. She had been a fool to marry this man, she told herself at last, and a sullen discontent and rage, that had been of slow but certain growth, made her long to free herself from this unprofitable hindrance for a time, at any rate. Go to sea? Yes, that was the best thing that could happen. Perhaps when he had worked hard a while on schooner fare, he would come home and be good for something!

Jerry finished his dinner in the course of time, and then sought his wife. It was not like her to go away in this silent fashion. Of late her gift of speech had been proved sufficiently formidable, and yet she had never looked so resolutely angry as to-day.

"Nancy," he began,—"Nancy, girl! I ain't goin' off to leave you, if your heart's set aginst it. I'll spudge up and take right holt."

But the wife turned slowly from the fence and faced him. Her eyes looked as if she had been crying. "You need n't stay on my account," she said. "I'll go right to work an' fit ye out. I'm sick of your meechin' talk, and I don't want to hear no more of it. Ef *I* was a man"—

Jerry Lane looked crestfallen for a minute or two; but when his stern partner in life had disappeared within the house, he slunk away among the apple-trees of the little orchard, and sat down on the grass in a shady spot. It was getting to be warm weather, but he would go round and hoe the old girl's garden stuff by and by. There would be something going on aboard the schooner, and with delicious anticipation of future pleasure the delinquent Jerry struck his knee with his hand, as if he were clapping a crony on the shoulder. He also winked several times at the same fancied companion. Then, with a comfortable chuckle, he laid himself down, and pulled his old hat over his eyes, and went to sleep, while the weeds grew at their own sweet will, and the currant worms went looping and devouring from twig to twig.

III

Summer went by, and winter began, and Mr. Jerry Lane did not reappear. He had promised to return in September when he parted from his wife early in June, for Nancy had relented a little at the last, and sorrowed at the prospect of so long a separation. She had already learned the vacillations and uncertainties of her husband's character; but though she accepted the truth that her marriage had been in every way a piece of foolishness, she still clung affectionately to his assumed fondness for her. She could not believe that this marriage was only one of his makeshifts, and that as soon as he grew tired of the constraint he would be ready to throw the benefits of respectable home life to the four winds. A little sentimental speech-making and a few kisses the morning he went away, and the gratitude he might well have shown for her generous care-taking and provision for his voyage won her soft heart back again, and made poor, elderly, simple-hearted Nancy watch him cross the marshes with tears and foreboding. If she could have called him back that day, she would have done so and been thankful. And all summer and winter, whenever the wind blew and thrashed the drooping elm boughs against the low roof over her head, she was as full of fears and anxieties as if Jerry were her only son and making his first voyage at sea. The neighbors pitied her for her disappointment. They liked Nancy; but they could not help saying, "I told you so." It would have been impossible not to respect the brave way in which she met the world's eye, and carried herself with innocent unconsciousness of having committed so laughable and unrewarding a folly. The loafers on the store steps had been unwontedly diverted one day, when Jerry, who was their chief wit and spokesman, rose slowly from his place, and said in pious tones, "Boys, I must go this minute. Grandma will keep dinner waiting." Mrs. Ann Lane did not show in her aging face how young her heart was, and after the schooner Susan Barnes had departed she seemed to pass swiftly from middle life and an almost youthful vigor to early age and a look of spent strength and dissatisfaction. "I suppose he did find it stupid," she assured herself, with wistful yearning for his rough words of praise, when she sat down alone to her dinner, or looked up sadly from her work, and missed the amusing though unedifying conversation he was wont to offer on stormy winter nights. How many of his marvelous tales were true she never cared to ask. He had come and gone, and she forgave him his shortcomings, and longed for his society with a heavy heart.

One spring day there was news in the Boston paper of the loss of the schooner Susan Barnes with all on board, and Nancy Lane's best friends shook their sage heads, and declared that as far as regarded that idle vagabond, Jerry Lane, it was all for the best. Nobody was interested in any other member of the crew, so the misfortune of the Susan Barnes seemed of but slight consequence in Walpole, she having passed out of her former owners' hands the autumn before. Jerry had stuck by the ship; at least, so he had sent word then to his wife by Skipper Nathan Low. The Susan Barnes was to sail regularly between Shediac and Newfoundland, and Jerry sent five dollars to Nancy, and promised to pay her a visit soon. "Tell her I'm layin' up somethin' handsome," he told the skipper with a grin, "and I've got some folks in Newfoundland I'll visit with on this voyage, and then I'll come ashore for good and farm it."

Mrs. Lane took the five dollars from the skipper as proudly as if Jerry had done the same thing so many times before that she hardly noticed it. The skipper gave the messages from Jerry, and felt that he had done the proper thing. When the news came

long afterward that the schooner was lost, that was
the next thing that Nancy knew about her wandering mate; and after the minister had come solemnly
to inform her of her bereavement, and had gone
away again, and she sat down and looked her wid-
owhood in the face, there was not a sadder nor a
lonelier woman in the town of Walpole.

All the neighbors came to condole with our hero-
ine, and, though nobody was aware of it, from that
time she was really happier and better satisfied with
life than she had ever been before. Now that she had
an ideal Jerry Lane to mourn over and think about,
to cherish and admire, she was day by day slowly forgetting the trouble he had been and the bitter shame
of him, and exalting his memory to something near
saintliness. "He meant well," she told herself again
and again. She thought nobody could tell so good a
story; she felt that with her own bustling, capable
ways he had no chance to do much that he might
have done. She had been too quick with him, and
alas, alas! how much better she would know how to
treat him if she could only see him again! A sense
of relief at his absence made her continually assure
herself of her great loss; and, false even to herself,
she mourned her sometime lover diligently, and
tried to think herself a broken-hearted woman. It
was thought among those who knew Nancy Lane
best that she would recover her spirits in time, but
Jerry's wildest anticipations of a proper respect to

his memory were more than realized in the first two years after the schooner Susan Barnes went to the bottom of the sea. His wife mourned for the man he ought to have been, not for the real Jerry, but she had loved him enough in the beginning to make her own love a precious possession for all time to come. It did not matter much, after all, what manner of man he was; she had found in him something on which to spend her hoarded affection.

IV

Nancy Lane was a peaceable woman and a good neighbor, but she never had been able to get on with one fellow townswoman, and that was Mrs. Deacon Elton. They managed to keep each other provoked and teased from one year's end to the other, and each good soul felt herself under a moral microscope, and understood that she was judged by a not very lenient criticism and discussion. Mrs. Lane clad herself in simple black after the news came of her husband's timely death, and Mrs. Elton made one of her farewell pilgrimages to church to see the new-made widow walk up the aisle.

"She need n't tell me she lays that affliction so much to heart," the deacon's wife sniffed faintly, after her exhaustion had been met by proper treatment of camphor and a glass of currant wine, at the parsonage, where she rested a while after service.

"Nancy Floyd knows she 's well through with such a piece of nonsense. If I had had my health, I should have spoken with her and urged her not to take the step in the first place. She has n't spoken six beholden words to me since that vagabond come to Walpole. I dare say she may have heard something I said at the time she married. I declare for 't, I never was so outdone as when the deacon came home and informed me Nancy Floyd was going to be married. She let herself down too low to ever hold the place again that she used to hold in folks' minds. And it's my opinion," said the sharp-eyed little woman, "she ain't got through with her pay yet."

But Mrs. Elton did not half comprehend the unconscious prophecy with which her words were freighted.

The months passed by: summer and winter came and went, and even those few persons who were misled by Nancy Lane's stern visage and forbidding exterior into forgetting her kind heart were at last won over to friendliness by her renewed devotion to the sick and old people of the rural community. She was so tender to little children that they all loved her dearly. She was ready to go to any household that needed help, and in spite of her ceaseless industry with her needle she found many a chance to do good, and help her neighbors to lift and carry the burdens of their lives. She blossomed out suddenly into a lovely, painstaking eagerness to be of use; it seemed as if her affectionate heart, once made generous, must go on spending its wealth wherever it could find an excuse. Even Mrs. Elton herself was touched by her old enemy's evident wish to be friends, and said nothing more about poor Nancy's looking as savage as a hawk. The only thing to admit was the truth that her affliction had proved a blessing to her. And it was in a truly kind and compassionate spirit that, after hearing a shocking piece of news, the deacon's hysterical wife forbore to spread it far and wide through the town first, and went down to the Widow Lane's one September afternoon. Nancy was stitching busily upon the deacon's new coat, and looked up with a friendly smile as her guest came in, in spite of an instinctive shrug as she had seen her coming up the yard. The dislike of the poor souls for each other was deeper than their philosophy could reach.

Mrs. Elton spent some minutes in the unnecessary endeavor to regain her breath, and to her surprise found she must make a real effort before she could tell her unwelcome news. She had been so full of it all the way from home that she had rehearsed the whole interview; now she hardly knew how to begin. Nancy looked serener than usual, but there was something wistful about her face as she glanced across the room, presently, as if to understand the reason of the long pause. The clock ticked loudly; the kitten clattered a spool against the table-leg, and had begun to snarl the thread round her busy paws, and Nancy looked down and saw her; then the instant consciousness of there being some unhappy reason for Mrs. Elton's call made her forget the creature's mischief, and anxiously lay down her work to listen.

"Capt'in Nathan Low was to our house to dinner," the guest began. "He's bargaining with the deacon about some hay. He's got a new schooner, Capt'in Nathan has, and is going to build up a regular business of freighting hay to Boston by sea. There's no market to speak of about here, unless you haul it way over to Downer, and you can't make but one turn a day."

" 'T would be a good thing," replied Nancy, trying to think that this was all, and perhaps the deacon wanted to hire her own field another year. He had underpaid her once, and they had not been on particularly good terms ever since. She would make her own bargains with Skipper Low, she thanked him and his wife!

"He's been down to the provinces these two or three years back, you know," the whining voice went on, and straightforward Ann Lane felt the old animosity rising within her. "At dinner-time I wa'n't able to eat much of anything, and so I was talking with Capt'in Nathan, and asking him some questions about them parts; and I expressed something about the mercy 't was his life should ha' been spared when that schooner, the Susan Barnes, was lost so quick after he sold out his part of her. And I put in a word, bein' 's we were neighbors, about how edifyin' your course had be'n under affliction. I noticed then he'd looked sort o'queer whilst I was talkin', but there was all the folks to the table, and you know he's a very cautious man, so he spoke of somethin' else. 'T wa'n't half an hour after dinner, I was comin' in with some plates and cups, tryin' to help what my stren'th would let me, and says he, 'Step out a little ways into the piece with me, Mis' Elton. I want to have a word with ye.' I went, too, spite o' my neuralgy, for I saw he'd got somethin' on his mind. 'Look here,' says he, 'I gathered from the way you spoke that Jerry Lane's wife expects he's dead.' Certain, says I, his name was in the list o' the Susan Barnes's crew, and we read it in the paper. 'No,' says he to me, 'he ran away the day they sailed; he wa'n't aboard, and he's livin' with another woman down to Shediac.' Them was his very words."

Nancy Lane sank back in her chair, and covered her horror-stricken eyes with her hands. "'T aint't pleasant news to have to tell," Sister Elton went on mildly, yet with evident relish and full command of the occasion. "He said he seen Jerry the morning he came away. I thought you ought to know it. I'll tell you one thing, Nancy: I told the skipper to keep still about it, and now I've told you, I won't spread it no further to set folks a-talking. I'll keep it secret till you say the word. There ain't much trafficking betwixt here and there, and he's dead to you, certain, as much as if he laid up here in the burying-ground."

Nancy had bowed her head upon the table; the thin sandy hair was streaked with gray. She did not answer one word; this was the hardest blow of all.

"I'm much obliged to you for being so friendly," she said after a few minutes, looking straight before her now in a dazed sort of way, and lifting the new coat from the floor, where it had fallen. "Yes, he's dead to me,—worse than dead, a good deal," and her lip quivered. "I can't seem to bring my thoughts to bear. I've got so used to thinkin'—No, don't you say nothin' to the folks yet. I'd do as much for you." And Mrs. Elton knew that the smitten fellow-creature before her spoke the truth, and forebore.

Two or three days came and went, and with every hour the quiet, simple-hearted woman felt more grieved and unsteady in mind and body. Such a shattering thunderbolt of news rarely falls into a human life. She could not sleep; she wandered to and fro in the little house, and cried until she could cry no longer. Then a great rage spurred and excited her. She would go to Shediac, and call Jerry Lane to account. She would accuse him face to face; and the woman whom he was deceiving, as perhaps he had deceived her, should know the baseness and cowardice of this miserable man. So, dressed in her respectable Sunday clothes, in the gray bonnet and shawl that never had known any journeys except to meeting, or to a country funeral or quiet holiday-making, Nancy Lane trusted herself for the first time to the bewildering railway, to the temptations and dangers of the wide world outside the bounds of Walpole.

Two or three days later still, the quaint, thin figure familiar in Walpole highways flitted down the street of a provincial town. In the most primitive region of China this woman could hardly have felt a greater sense of foreign life and strangeness. At another time her native good sense and shrewd observation would have delighted in the experiences of this first week of travel, but she was too sternly angry and aggrieved, too deeply plunged in a survey of her own calamity, to take much notice of what was going on about her. Later she condemned the unworthy folly of the whole errand, but in these days the impulse to seek the culprit and confront him was irresistible.

The innkeeper's wife, a kindly creature, urged this puzzling guest to wait and rest and eat some supper, but Nancy refused, and without asking her way left the brightly lighted, flaring little public room, where curious eyes already offended her, and went out into the damp twilight. The voices of the street boys sounded outlandish, and she felt more and more lonely. She longed for Jerry to appear for protection's sake: she forgot why she sought him, and was eager to shelter herself behind the flimsy bulwark of his manhood. She rebuked herself presently with terrible bitterness for a womanish wonder whether he would say, " Why, Nancy, girl!" and be glad to see her. Poor woman, it was a work-laden, serious girlhood that had been hers, at any rate. The power of giving her whole self in unselfish, enthusiastic, patient devotion had not belonged to her youth only; it had sprung fresh and blossoming in her heart as every new year came and went.

One might have seen her stealing through the shadows, skirting the edge of a lumberyard, step-ping among the refuse of the harbor side, asking a question timidly now and then of some passer-by. Yes, they knew Jerry Lane,—his house was only a little way off; and one curious and compassionate Scotchman, divining by some inner sense the exciting nature of the errand, turned back, and offered fruitlessly to go with the stranger. "You know the man?" he asked. "He is his own enemy, but doing better now that he is married. He minds his work, I know that well; and he's taken a good wife." Nancy's heart beat faster with honest pride for a moment, until the shadow of the ugly truth and reality made it sink back to heaviness, and the fire of her smouldering rage was again kindled. She would speak to Jerry face to face before she slept, and a horrible contempt and scorn were

ready for him, as with a glance either way along the
road she entered the narrow yard, and went noise-
lessly toward the window of a low, poor-looking
house, from whence a bright light was shining out
into the night.

Yes, there was Jerry, and it seemed as if she must
faint and fall at the sight of him. How young he
looked still! The thought smote her like a blow.
They never were mates for each other, Jerry and she.
Her own life was waning; she was an old woman.

He never had been so thrifty and respectable
before; the other woman ought to know the savage
truth about him, for all that! But at that moment the
other woman stooped beside the supper table, and
lifted a baby from its cradle, and put the dear, live
little thing into its father's arms. The baby was
wide-awake, and laughed at Jerry, who laughed back
again, and it reached up to catch at a handful of the
curly hair which had been poor Nancy's delight.

The other woman stood there looking at them,
full of pride and love. She was young, and trig, and
neat. She looked a brisk, efficient little creature.
Perhaps Jerry would make something of himself
now; he always had it in him. The tears were running down Nancy's cheeks; the rain, too, had begun
to fall. She stood there watching the little household sit down to supper, and noticed with eager
envy how well cooked the food was, and how hun-
grily the master of the house ate what was put

before him. All thoughts of ending the new wife's sin and folly vanished away. She could not enter in and break another heart; hers was broken already, and it would not matter. And Nancy Lane, a widow indeed, crept away again, as silently as she had come, to think what was best to be done, to find alternate woe and comfort in the memory of the sight she had seen.

The little house at the edge of the Walpole marshes seemed full of blessed shelter and comfort the evening that its forsaken mistress came back to it. Her strength was spent; she felt much more desolate now that she had seen with her own eyes that Jerry Lane was alive than when she had counted him among the dead. An uncharacteristic disregard of the laws of the land filled this good woman's mind. Jerry had his life to live, and she wished him no harm. She wondered often how the baby grew, and fancied again and again the changes and conditions of the far-away household. Alas! she knew only too well the weakness of the man, and once she exclaimed, in a grim outburst of impatience, "I'd rather others should have to cope with him than me!"

But that evening, when she came back from She-diac, and sat in the dark for a long time, lest Mrs. Elton should see the light and risk her life in the evening air to bring unwelcome sympathy,—that evening, I say, came the hardest moment of all, when

Ann Floyd, tailoress, of so many virtuous, self-respecting years, whose idol had turned to clay, who was shamed, disgraced, and wronged, sat down alone to supper in the little kitchen.

She had put one cup and saucer on the table and then stood and looked at them through bitter tears. Somehow a consciousness of her solitary age, her uncompanioned future, rushed through her mind; the failure of her best earthly hope was enough to break a stronger woman's heart.

Who can laugh at my Marsh Rosemary, or who can cry, for that matter? The gray primness of the plant is made up from a hundred colors if you look close enough to find them. This Marsh Rosemary stands in her own place, and holds her dry leaves and tiny blossoms steadily toward the same sun that the pink lotus blooms for, and the white rose.

Young Goodman Brown

[N A T H A N I E L   H A W T H O R N E]

Young Goodman Brown came forth at sunset into the street of Salem village, put his head back, after crossing the threshold, to exchange a parting kiss with his young wife. And Faith, as the wife was aptly named, thrust her own pretty head into the street, letting the wind play with the pink ribbons of her cap, while she called to Goodman Brown.

"Dearest heart," whispered she, softly and rather sadly, when her lips were close to his ear, "prythee, put off your journey until sunrise and sleep in your own bed to-night. A lone woman is troubled with such dreams and such thoughts that she's afeard of herself sometimes. Pray tarry with me this night, dear husband, of all nights in the year."

"My love and my Faith," replied young Goodman Brown, "of all nights in the year, this one must I tarry away from thee. My journey, as thou callest it, forth and back again, must needs be done 'twixt now and sunrise. What, my sweet, pretty wife! Doest thou doubt me already, and we but three months married?"

"Then God bless you," said Faith with the pink ribbons, "and may you find all well when you come back!"

"Amen!" cried Goodman Brown. "Say thy prayers, dear Faith, and go to bed at dusk, and no harm will come to thee."

So they parted, and the young man pursued his way until, being about to turn the corner by the meeting-house, he looked back and saw the head of Faith still peeping after him with a melancholy air, in spite of her pink ribbons.

"Poor little Faith!" thought he, for his heart smote him. "What a wretch am I, to leave her on such an errand. She talks of dreams, too. Methought, as she spoke, there was trouble in her face, as if a dream had warned her what work is to be done to-night. But no, no! 'twould kill her to think it. Well, she's a blessed angel on earth, and after this one night I'll cling to her skirts and follow her to heaven."

With this excellent resolve for the future, Goodman Brown felt himself justified in making more haste on his present evil purpose. He had then taken a dreary road darkened by all the gloomiest trees of the forest, which barely stood aside to let the narrow path creep through, and closed immediately behind. It was all as lonely as could be; and there is this peculiarity in such a solitude— that the traveler knows not who may be concealed by the innumerable trunks and the thick boughs overhead, so that with lonely footsteps he may yet be passing through an unseen multitude.

"There may be a devilish Indian behind every tree," said Goodman Brown to himself; and he glanced fearfully behind him as he added: "What if the devil himself should be at my very elbow?"

His head being turned back, he passed a crook of the road, and, looking forward again, beheld the figure of a man in grave and decent attire seated at the foot of an old tree. He arose at Goodman's approach, and walked onward side by side with him.

"You are late, Goodman Brown." said he. "The clock of the Old South was striking as I came through Boston, and that is full fifteen minutes agone."

"Faith kept me back awhile," replied the young man, with a tremor in his voice caused by the sudden appearance of his companion, though not wholly unexpected.

It was now deep dusk in the forest, and deepest in that part of it where these two were journeying. As nearly as could be discerned, the second traveler was about 50 years old, apparently in the same rank of life as Goodman Brown, and bearing a considerable resemblance to him, though perhaps more in expression than features. Still they might have been taken for father and son. And yet, though the elder person was as simply clad as the younger, and as simple in manner too, he had an indescribable air of one who knew the world, and would have felt abashed at the governor's dinner-table or in King William's court were it possible that his affairs should call him thither. But the only thing about him that could be fixed upon as remarkable was his staff, which bore the likeness of a great black snake so curiously wrought that it might almost be seen to twist and wriggle itself like a living serpent. This, of course, must have been an ocular deception, assisted by the uncertain light.

"Come, Goodman Brown!" cried his fellow-traveler; "this a dull pace for the beginning of a journey. Take my staff, if you are so soon weary."

"Friend," said the other, exchanging his slow pace for a full stop, "having kept covenant by meeting thee here, it is my purpose now to return from whence I came. I have scruples touching the matter thou wotst of."

"Sayest thou so?" replied he of the serpent, smiling apart. "Let us walk on, nevertheless, reasoning as we go, and if I convince thee not, thou shalt turn back. We are but a little way in the forest yet."

"Too far—too far!" exclaimed the good man, unconsciously resuming his walk. "My father never went into the woods on such an errand, nor his father before him. We have been a race of honest men and good Christians since the days of the martyrs, and shall I be the first of the name of Brown that ever took this path and kept—"

"'Such company,' thou wouldst say," observed the elder person, interrupting his pause. "Well said, Goodman Brown! I have been as well acquainted with your family as with ever a one among the puritans, and that's no trifle to say. I helped your grandfather the constable when he lashed the quaker woman so smartly through the streets of Salem, and it was I who brought your father a pitch-pine knot kindled at my own hearth to set fire to an Indian village in King Philip's war. They were my good friends, both, and many a pleasant walk have we had along this path, and returned merrily after midnight. I would fain be friends with you for their sake."

"If it be as thou sayest," replied Goodman Brown, "I marvel they never spoke of these matters. Or, verily, I marvel not, seeing that the least rumor of the sort would have driven them from England. We are a people of prayer and good works to boot, and abide no such wickedness."

"Wickedness or not," said the traveler with the twisted staff, "I have a very general acquaintance here in New England. The deacons of many a church have drunk the communion wine with me, the selectmen of divers towns make me their chairman, and a majority of the great and general court are firm supporters of my interest. The governor and I, too—But these are state secrets."

"Can this be so?" cried Goodman Brown, with a stare of amazement at his undisturbed companion. "Howbeit, I have nothing to do with the governor and council; they have their own ways, and are no rule for a simple husband-man like me. But were I to go on with thee, how could I meet the eye of that good old man our minister at Salem village? Oh, his voice would make me tremble both Sabbath-day and lecture-day."

Thus far the elder traveler had listened with due gravity, but now burst into a fit of irrepressible mirth, shaking himself so violently that his snake-like staff actually seemed to wriggle in sympathy.

"Ha! ha! ha!" shouted he, again and again; then, composing himself: "Well, go on, Goodman Brown, go on; but prythee don't kill me with laughing!"

"Well, then, to end the matter at once," said Goodman Brown, considerably nettled, "there is my wife, Faith. It would break her dear little heart, and I'd rather break my own."

"Nay, if that be the case," answered the other, "e'en go thy ways, Goodman Brown. I would not for twenty old women like the one hobbling before us that Faith should come to any harm."

As he spoke he pointed his staff at a female figure on the path, in whom Goodman Brown recognized a very pious and exemplary dame who had taught him his catechism in youth, and was still his moral and spiritual adviser jointly with the minister and Deacon Gookin.

"A marvel, truly, that Goody Cloyse should be so far in the wilderness at nightfall," said he. "But, with your leave, friend, I shall take a cut through the woods until we have left this Christian woman behind. Being a stranger to you she might ask whom I was consorting with and whither I was going."

"Be it so," said his fellow-traveler. "Betake you to the woods and let me keep the path."

Accordingly, the young man turned aside, but took care to watch his companion, who advanced softly along the road until he had come within a staff's length of the old dame. She, meanwhile, was making the best of her way with singular speed for so aged a woman and mumbling some indistinct words—a prayer, doubtless—as she went. The traveler put forth his staff and touched her withered neck with what seemed the serpent's tail.

"The devil!" screamed the pious old lady.

"Then Goody Cloyse knows her old friend?" observed the traveler, confronting her and leaning on his writhing stick.

"Ah, forsooth! and is it your worship, indeed?" cried the good dame. "Yea, truly is it, and in the very image of my old gossip Goodman Brown, the grandfather of the silly fellow that now is. But would your worship believe it? My broomstick hath strangely disappeared—stolen as I suspect, by that unhanged witch Goody Cory, and that too, when I was all anointed with the juice of smallage and cinque-foil and wolf's-bane—"

"Mingled with fine wheat and the fat of a new-born babe," said the shape of old Goodman Brown.

"Ah! your worship knows the recipe," cried the old lady, cackling aloud. "So, as I was saying, being all ready for the meeting, and no horse to ride on, I made up my mind to foot it; for they tell me there is a nice young man to be taken into communion to-night. But now your good worship will lend me your arm and we shall be there in a twinkling."

"That can hardly be," answered her friend. "I may not spare you my arm, Goody Cloyse, but here is my staff, if you will."

So saying, he threw it down at her feet, where, perhaps, it assumed life, being one of the rods which its owner had formerly lent to the Egyptian magi. Of this fact, however, Goodman Brown could not take cognizance. He had cast up his eyes in aston-ishment, and, looking down again, beheld neither Goody Cloyse nor the serpentine staff, but his fellow-traveler alone, who waited for him as calmly as if nothing had happened.

"That old woman taught me my catechism!" said the young man; and there was a world of meaning in this simple comment.

They continued to walk onward, while the elder traveler exhorted his companion to make good speed and persevere in the path, discoursing so aptly that his arguments seemed rather to spring up in the bosom of his auditor than to be suggested by himself. As they went he plucked a branch of maple, to serve for a walking-stick, and began to strip it of the twigs and little boughs, which were wet with evening dew. The moment his fingers touched them they became strangely withered and dried up, as with a week's sunshine. Thus the pair proceeded at a good free pace until suddenly in a gloomy hollow of the road, Goodman Brown sat himself down on the stump of a tree and refused to go any farther.

"Friend," said he, stubbornly, "my mind is made up. Not another step will I budge on this errand. What if a wretched old woman do choose to go to the devil, when I thought she was going to heaven? Is that any reason why I should quit my dear faith and go after her?"

"You will think better of this by and by," said his acquaintance, composedly. "Sit here and rest yourself awhile; and when you feel like moving again, there is my staff to help you along." Without more words he threw his companion the maple stick, and was as speedily out of sight as if he had vanished into the deepening gloom.

The young man sat a few moments by the roadside, applauding himself greatly and thinking with how clear a conscience he should meet the minister in his morning walk, nor shrink from the eye of good old Deacon Gookin. And what calm sleep would be his that very night, which was to have been spent so wickedly, but purely and sweetly now in the arms of Faith? Amid these pleasant and praiseworthy meditations Goodman Brown heard the tramp of horses along the road, and deemed it advisable to conceal himself within the verge of the forest, conscious of the guilty purpose that had brought him thither, though now so happily turned from it.

On came the hoof-tramps and the voices of the riders—two grave old voices conversing soberly as they drew near. These mingled sounds appeared to pass along the road within a few yards of the young man's hiding-place, but, owing, doubtless, to the depth of the gloom at that particular spot, neither the travelers nor their steeds were visible. Though their figures brushed the small boughs by the way-side, it could not be seen that they intercepted even for a moment the faint gleam from the strip of bright sky athwart which they must have passed. Goodman Brown alternately crouched and stood on tip-toe, pulling aside the branches and thrusting forth his head as far as he dare, without discerning so much as a shadow. It vexed him the more because he could have sworn, were such a thing possible, that he recognized the voices of the minister and

Deacon Gookin jogging along quietly, as they were wont to do when bound to some ordination or ecclesiastical council. While yet within hearing one of the riders stopped to pluck a switch.

"Of the two, reverend sir," said the voice like the deacon's, "I had rather miss an ordination dinner than to-night's meeting. They tell me that some of our community are to be here from Falmouth and beyond, and others from Connecticut and Rhode Island, besides several of the Indian pow-wows, who after their fashion knew almost as much deviltry as the best of us. Moreover, there is a goodly young woman to be taken into communion."

"Mighty well, Deacon Gookin!" replied the solemn old tones of the minister. "Spur up, or we shall be late. Nothing can be done, you know, until I get on the ground."

The hoofs clattered again, and the voices talking so strangely in the empty air passed on through the forest, where no church had ever been gathered nor solitary Christian prayed. Whither, then, could these holy men be journeying so deep into the heathen wilderness? Young Goodman Brown caught hold of a tree for support, being ready to sink down on the ground, faint and overburdened with the heavy sickness of his heart. He looked up to the sky, doubting whether there really was a heaven above him; yet there was the blue arch and the stars brightening in it.

"With heaven above and Faith below, I will yet stand firm against the devil!" cried Goodman Brown.

While he still gazed upward into the deep arch of the firmament and had lifted his hands to pray, a cloud—though no wind was stirring—hurried across the zenith and hid the brightening stars. The blue sky was still visible except directly over-head, where this black mass of cloud was sweeping swiftly northward. Aloft in the air, as if from the depths of the cloud, came a confused and doubt-ful sound of voices. Once the listener fancied that he could distinguish the accents of towns-people of his own men and women, both pious and ungodly, many of whom he had met at the com-munion-table, and had seen others rioting at the tavern. The next moment, so indistinct were the sounds, he doubted whether he had heard aught but the murmur of the old forest whispering without a wind. Then came a stronger swell of those familiar tones heard daily in the sunshine at Salem village, but never until now from a cloud of night. There was one voice of a young woman uttering lamentations, yet with an uncertain sor-row, and entreating for some favor which perhaps it would grieve her to obtain. And all the unseen multitude, both saints and sinnners, seemed to encourage her onward.

"Faith!" shouted Goodman Brown, in a voice of agony and desperation; and the echoes of the forest

mocked him, crying: "Faith! Faith!" as if bewildered wretches were seeking her all through the
wilderness.

The cry of grief, rage and terror was yet piercing
the night, when the unhappy husband held his
breath for a response. There was a scream, drowned
immediately in a louder murmur of voices fading
into far off laughter, as the dark cloud swept away,
leaving the clear and silent sky above Goodman
Brown. But something fluttered lightly down
through the air and caught on the branch of a tree.
The young man seized it and beheld a pink ribbon.

"My Faith is gone!" cried he, after one stupefied
moment. "There is no good on earth, and sin is but
a name! Come, devil, for to thee is this world given!"

And maddened with despair, so that he laughed
loud and long, did Goodman Brown grasp his staff
and set forth again at such a rate that he seemed to
fly along the forest-path rather than to walk or
run. The road grew wilder and drearier and more
faintly traced, and vanished at length, leaving him
in the heart of the dark wilderness, still rushing
onward with the instinct that guides mortal man to
evil. The whole forest was peopled with frightful
sounds—the creaking of the trees, the howling of
wild beasts and the yell of Indians—while sometimes the wind tolled like a distant church-bell,
and sometimes gave a broad roar around the traveler, as if all nature were laughing him to scorn.

But he was himself the chief horror on the scene, and shrank not from its other horrors.

"Ha! ha! ha!" roared Goodman Brown, when the wind laughed at him. "Let us hear which will laugh loudest; think not to frighten me with your deviltry! Come, witch! come, wizard! come, Indian pow-wow! come, devil himself! And here comes Goodman Brown. You may as well fear him as he fear you."

In truth, all through the haunted forest there could be nothing more frightful than the figure of Goodman Brown. On he flew among the black pines, brandishing his staff with frenzied gestures, now giving vent to an inspiration of horrid blasphemy, and now shouting forth such laughter as set all the echoes of the forest laughing like demons around him. The fiend in his own shape is less hideous than when he rages in the breast of man. Thus sped the demoniac on his course, until, quivering among the trees, he saw a red light before him, as when the felled trunks and branches of a clearing have been set on fire and throw up their lurid blaze against the sky at the hour of midnight. He paused in a lull of the tempest that had driven him onward, and heard the swell of what seemed a hymn rolling solemnly from a distance with the weight of many voices. He knew the tune; it was a familiar one in the choir of the village meeting-house. The verse died heavily away and was lengthened by a chorus, not of human voices, but of all the sounds of the benighted wilderness pealing in awful harmony together. Goodman Brown cried out and his cry was lost to his own ear by its unison with the cry of the desert.

In the interval of silence he stole forward until the light glared full upon his eyes. At one extremity of an open space hemmed in by the dark wall of the forest arose a rock bearing some rude natural resemblance either to an altar or a pulpit and surrounded by four blazing pines, their tops aflame, their stems untouched, like candles at an evening meeting. The mass of foliage that had overgrown the summit of the rock was all on fire, blazing high into the night and fitfully illuminating the whole field. Each pendant twig and leafy festoon was in a blaze. As the red light arose and fell a numerous congregation alternately shone forth, then disappeared in shadow and again grew, as it were, out of the darkness, peopling the heart of the solitary woods at once.

"A grave and dark-clad company!" quoth Goodman Brown.

In truth, they were such. Among them, quivering to and fro between gloom and splendor, appeared faces that would be seen next day at the council-board of the province and others which Sabbath after Sabbath looked devoutly heavenward and benignantly over the crowded pews from the holiest pulpits in the land. Some affirm that the lady of the governor was there. At least, there were high dames well known to her and wives of honored husbands and widows a great multitude and ancient maidens all of excellent repute and fair young girls who trembled lest their mothers should espy them. Either the sudden gleams of light flashing over the obscure field bedazzled Goodman Brown or he recognized a score of the church-members of Salem village famous for their especial sanctity. Good old Deacon Gookin had arrived and waited at the skirts of that venerable saint his reverend pastor. But irreverently consorting with these grave, reputable and pious people, these elders of the church, these chaste dames and dewy virgins, there were men of dissolute lives and women of spotted fame—wretches given over to all mean and filthy vice and suspected even of horrid crimes. It was strange to see that the good shrank not from the wicked, nor were the sinners abashed by the saints. Scattered, also, among their pale-faced enemies were the Indian priests, or pow-wows, who had often scared their native forest with more hideous incantations than any known to English witchcraft.

"But where is Faith?" thought Goodman Brown, and as hope came into his heart he trembled.

Another verse of the hymn arose, a slow and mournful strain such as the pious love, but joined to words which expressed all that our nature can conceive of sin and darkly hinted at far more.

Unfathomable to mere mortals is the lore of fiends. Verse after verse was sung and still the chorus of the desert swelled between like the deepest tone of a mighty organ. And with the final peal of that dreadful anthem there came a sound as if the roaring wind, the rushing streams, the howling beasts and every other voice of the unconverted wilderness, were mingling and according with the voice of guilty man in homage to the prince of all. The four blazing pines threw up a loftier flame and obscurely discovered shapes and visages of horror on the smoke-wreaths above the impious assembly. At the same moment the fire on the rock shot redly forth and formed a glowing arch above its base, where now appeared a figure. With reverence be it spoken, the apparition bore no slight similitude, both in garb and manner, to some grave divine of the New England churches.

"Bring forth the converts!" cried a voice that echoed through the field and rolled into the forest.

At the word Goodman Brown stepped forth from the shadow of the trees and approached the congregation, with whom he felt a loathful brotherhood by the sympathy of all that was wicked in his heart. He could have well-nigh sworn that the shape of his own dead father beckoned him to advance, looking downward from a smoke-wreath, while a woman with dim features of despair threw out her hand to warn him back. Was it his mother? But he had no power to retreat one step nor to resist even in thought when the minister and good old Deacon Gookin seized his arms and led him to the blazing rock. Thither came, also, the slender form of a veiled female, led between Goody Cloyse, that pious teacher of the catechism, and Martha Carrier, who had received the devil's promise to be queen of hell. A rampant hag was she! And there stood the proselytes, beneath the canopy of fire.

"Welcome, my children," said the dark figure, "to the communion of your race! Ye have found thus young your nature and your destiny. My children, look behind you!"

They turned, and, flashing forth, as it were, in a sheet of flame, the fiend-worshipers were seen; the smile of welcome gleamed darkly on every visage.

"There," resumed the sable form, "are all whom ye have reverenced from youth. Ye deemed them holier than yourselves and shrank from your own sin, contrasting it with their lives of righteousness and prayerful aspirations heavenward. Yet here are they all in my worshiping assembly! This night it shall be granted you to know their secret deeds— how hoary-bearded elders of the church have whispered wanton words to the young maids of their households, how many a woman eager for widow's weeds has given her husband a drink at bedtime and let him sleep his last sleep in her bosom, how beardless youths have made haste to inherit their father's wealth, and how fair damsels—blush not, sweet ones! have dug little graves in the garden and bidden me, the sole guest, to an infant's funeral. By the sympathy of your human hearts for sin ye shall scent out all the places—whether in church, bedchamber, street, field or forest—where crime has been committed, and shall exult to behold the whole earth one stain of guilt, one mighty blood-spot. Far more than this; it shall be yours to penetrate in every bosom the deep mystery of sin, the fountain of all wicked arts, and which inexhaustibly supplies more evil impulses than human power—than my power at its utmost—can make manifest in deeds. And now, my children, look upon each other."

They did so, and by the blaze of the hell-kindled torches the wretched man beheld his Faith, and the wife her husband, trembling before that unhallowed altar.

"Lo! there ye stand, my children," said the figure, in a deep and solemn tone almost sad with its despairing awfulness, as if his once angelic nature could yet mourn for our miserable race. "Depending upon one another's hearts, ye had still hoped that virtue were not all a dream; now are ye undeceived. Evil is the nature of mankind; evil must be your only happiness. Welcome, again, my children, to the communion of your race!"

"Welcome!" repeated the fiend-worshipers, in one cry of despair and triumph.

And there they stood, the only pair, as it seemed, who were yet hesitating on the verge of wickedness in this dark world. A basin was hollowed naturally in the rock. Did it contain water reddened by the lurid light? or was it blood, or perchance a liquid flame? Herein did the Shape of Evil dip his hand and prepare to lay the mark of baptism upon their foreheads, that they might be partakers of the mystery of sin, more conscious of the secret guilt of others, both in deed and thought, than they could now be of their own. The husband cast one look at his pale wife, and Faith at him. What polluted wretches would the next glance show them to each other, shuddering alike at what they disclosed and what they saw!

"Faith! Faith!" cried the husband. Look up to heaven and resist the wicked one!"

Whether Faith obeyed he knew not. Hardly had he spoken when he found himself amid calm night and solitude listening to a roar of the wind which died heavily away through the forest. He staggered against the rock and felt it chill and damp, while a hanging twig that had been all on fire besprinkled his cheek with the coldest dew.

The next morning young Goodman Brown came slowly into the street of Salem village staring around him like a bewildered man. The good old minister was taking a walk along the grave-yard to get an appetite for breakfast and meditate his sermon, and bestowed a blessing as be passed on Goodman Brown; he shrank from the venerable saint as if to avoid an anathema. Old Deacon Gookin was at domestic worship, and the holy words of his prayer were heard through the open window: "What God doth the wizard pray to?" quoth Goodman Brown. Goody Cloyse, that excellent old Christian, stood in the early sunshine at her own lattice catechising a little girl who had brought her a pint of morning's milk; Goodman Brown snatched away the child as from the grasp of the fiend himself. Turning the corner by the meeting-house he spied the head of Faith, with the pink ribbons, gazing anxiously forth, and bursting into such joy at sight of him that she skipped along the street and almost kissed her husband before the whole village; but Goodman Brown looked sternly and sadly into her face and passed on without a greeting.

Had Goodman Brown fallen asleep in the forest and only dreamed a wild dream of a witch meeting? Be it so, if you will. But, alas! it was a dream of evil omen for young Goodman Brown. A stern, a sad, a darkly meditative, a distrustful, if not a desperate, man did he become from the night of that fearful dream. On the Sabbath day when the congregation was singing a holy psalm he could not listen because an anthem of sin rushed loudly upon his ear and drowned all the blessed strain. When the minister spoke from the pulpit with power and fervid eloquence and with his hand on the open bible of the sacred truths of our religion and of saint-like lives and triumphant deaths and of future bliss or misery unutterable, then did Goodman Brown turn pale, dreading lest the roof should thunder down upon the gray blasphemer and his hearers. Often, awaking suddenly at midnight, he shrank from the bosom of Faith, and at morning or eventide when the family knelt down at prayer he scowled and muttered to himself and gazed sternly at his wife and turned away. And when he had lived long and was borne to his grave a hoary corpse, followed by Faith, an aged woman, and children and grandchildren, a goodly procession, besides neighbors not a few, they carved no hopeful verse upon his tombstone; for his dying hour was gloom.

Miss Mehetabel's Son

[**THOMAS BAILEY ALDRICH**]

I

THE OLD TAVERN AT BAYLEY'S FOUR-CORNERS

You will not find Greenton, or Bayley's Four-Corners as it is more usually designated, on any map of New England that I know of. It is not a town; it is not even a village; it is merely an absurd hotel. The almost indescribable place called Greenton is at the intersection of four roads, in the heart of New Hampshire, twenty miles from the nearest settlement of note, and ten miles from any railway station. A good location for a hotel, you will say. Precisely; but there has always been a hotel there, and for the last dozen years it has been pretty well patronized—by one boarder. Not to trifle with an intelligent public, I will state at once that, in the early part of this century, Greenton was a point at which the mail-coach, on the Great Northern Route, stopped to change horses and allow the passengers to dine. People in the county, wishing to take the early mail Portsmouth-ward, put up overnight at the old tavern, famous for its irreproachable larder and soft feather-beds. The tavern at that time was kept by Jonathan Bayley, who rivalled his wallet in growing corpulent, and in due time passed away. At his death the establishment, which included a farm, fell into the hands of a son-in-law. Now, though Bayley left his son-in-law a hotel,—which sounds handsome,—he left him no guests; for at about the period of the old man's death the old stage-coach died also. Apoplexy carried off one, and steam the other. Thus, by a sudden swerve in the tide of progress, the tavern at the Corners found itself high and dry, like a wreck on a sand-bank. Shortly after this event, or maybe contemporaneously, there was some attempt to build a town at Greenton; but it apparently failed, if eleven cellars choked up with *débris* and overgrown with burdocks are any indication of failure. The farm, however, was a good farm, as things go in New Hampshire; and Tobias Sewell, the son-in-law, could afford to snap his fingers at the travelling public if they came near enough,—which they never did.

The hotel remains to-day pretty much the same as when Jonathan Bayley handed in his accounts in

1840, except that Sewell has from time to time sold the furniture of some of the upper chambers to bridal couples in the neighborhood. The bar is still open, and the parlor door says PARLOUR in tall black letters. Now and then a passing drover looks in at that lonely bar-room, where a high-shouldered bottle of Santa Cruz rum ogles with a peculiarly knowing air a shrivelled lemon on a shelf; now and then a farmer comes across country to talk crops and stock and take a friendly glass with Tobias; and now and then a circus caravan with speckled ponies, or a menagerie with a soggy elephant, halts under the swinging sign, on which there is a dim mail-coach with four phantomish horses driven by a portly gentleman whose head has been washed off by the rain. Other customers there are none, except that one regular boarder whom I have mentioned.

If misery makes a man acquainted with strange bedfellows, it is equally certain that the profession of surveyor and civil engineer often takes one into undreamed-of localities. I had never heard of Greenton until my duties sent me there, and kept me there two weeks in the dreariest season of the year. I do not think I would, of my own volition, have selected Greenton for a fortnight's sojourn at any time; but now the business is over, I shall never regret the circumstances that made me the guest of Tobias Sewell and brought me into intimate relations with Miss Mehetabel's Son.

It was a black October night in the year of grace 1872, that discovered me standing in front of the old tavern at the Corners. Though the ten miles' ride from K—— had been depressing, especially the last five miles, on account of the cold autumnal rain that had set in, I felt a pang of regret on hearing the rickety open wagon turn round in the road and roll off in the darkness. There were no lights visible anywhere, and only for the big, shapeless mass of something in front of me, which the driver had said was the hotel, I should have fancied that I had been set down by the roadside. I was wet to the skin and in no amiable humor; and not being able to find bell-pull or knocker, or even a door, I belabored the side of the house with my heavy walking-stick. In a minute or two I saw a light flickering somewhere aloft, then I heard the sound of a window opening, followed by an exclamation of disgust as a blast of wind extinguished the candle which had given me an instantaneous picture *en silhouette* of a man leaning out of a casement.

"I say, what do you want, down there?" said an unprepossessing voice.

"I want to come in, I want a supper, and a bed, and numberless things."

"This is n't no time of night to go rousing honest folks out of their sleep. Who are you, anyway?"

The question, superficially considered, was a very simple one, and I, of all people in the world, ought to

have been able to answer it off-hand; but it staggered me. Strangely enough, there came drifting
across my memory the lettering on the back of a
metaphysical work which I had seen years before on
a shelf in the Astor Library. Owing to an unpremed-
itatedly funny collocation of title and author, the
lettering read as follows: "Who Am I? Jones." Evidently it had puzzled Jones to know who he was, or
he would n't have written a book about it, and come
to so lame and impotent a conclusion. It certainly
puzzled me at that instant to define my identity.
"Thirty years ago," I reflected, "I was nothing; fifty
years hence I shall be nothing again, humanly speaking. In the mean time, who am I, sure enough?" It
had never occurred to me before what an indefinite
article I was. I wish it had not occurred to me then.
Standing there in the rain and darkness, I wrestled
vainly with the problem, and was constrained to fall
back upon a Yankee expedient.

"Is n't this a hotel?" I asked finally.

"Well, it is a sort of hotel," said the voice, doubtfully. My hesitation and prevarication had apparently
not inspired my interlocutor with confidence in me.

"Then let me in. I have just driven over from
K—— in this infernal rain. I am wet through and
through."

"But what do you want here, at the Corners?
What's your business? People don't come here, least
ways in the middle of the night."

"It is n't in the middle of the night," I returned, incensed. "I come on business connected with the new road. I'm the superintendent of the works."

"Oh!"

"And if you don't open the door at once, I 'll raise the whole neighborhood,—and then go to the other hotel."

When I said that, I supposed Greenton was a village with three or four thousand population at least, and was wondering vaguely at the absence of lights and other signs of human habitation. Surely, I thought, all the people cannot be abed and asleep at half past ten o'clock: perhaps I am in the business section of the town, among the shops.

"You jest wait," said the voice above.

This request was not devoid of a certain accent of menace, and I braced myself for a sortie on the part of the besieged, if he had any such hostile intent. Presently a door opened at the very place where I least expected a door, at the farther end of the building, in fact, and a man in his shirt-sleeves, shielding a candle with his left hand, appeared on the threshold. I passed quickly into the house with Mr. Tobias Sewell (for this was Mr. Sewell) at my heels, and found myself in a long, low-studded bar-room.

There were two chairs drawn up before the hearth, on which a huge hemlock backlog was still smouldering, and on the unpainted deal counter contiguous stood two cloudy glasses with bits of lemon-peel in the bottom, hinting at recent libations. Against the discolored wall over the bar hung a yellowed hand-bill, in a warped frame, announcing that "the Next Annual N. H. Agricultural Fair" would take place on the 10th of September, 1841. There was no other furniture or decoration in this dismal apartment, except the cobwebs which festooned the ceiling, hanging down here and there like stalactites.

Mr. Sewell set the candlestick on the mantel-shelf, and threw some pine-knots on the fire, which immediately broke into a blaze, and showed him to be a lank, narrow-chested man, past sixty, with sparse, steel-gray hair, and small, deep-set eyes, per-fectly round, like a carp's, and of no particular color. His chief personal characteristics seemed to be too much feet and not enough teeth. His sharply cut, but rather simple face, as he turned it towards me, wore a look of interrogation. I replied to his mute inquiry by taking out my pocket-book and handing him my business-card, which he held up to the can-dle and perused with great deliberation.

"You 're a civil engineer, are you?" he said, dis-playing his gums, which gave his countenance an expression of almost infantile innocence. He made no further audible remark, but mumbled between his thin lips something which an imaginative person might have construed into, "If you' re a civil engi-neer, I' ll be blessed if I would n't like to see an uncivil one!"

Mr. Sewell's growl, however, was worse than his bite,—owing to his lack of teeth probably,—for he very good-naturedly set himself to work preparing supper for me. After a slice of cold ham, and a warm punch, to which my chilled condition gave a grateful flavor, I went to bed in a distant chamber in a most amiable mood, feeling satisfied that Jones was a donkey to bother himself about his identity.

When I awoke the sun was several hours high. My bed faced a window, and by raising myself on one elbow I could look out on what I expected would be the main street. To my astonishment I beheld a lonely country road winding up a sterile hill and disappearing over the ridge. In a cornfield at the right of the road was a small private graveyard enclosed by a crumbling stone-wall with a red gate. The only thing suggestive of life was this little corner lot occupied by death. I got out of bed and went to the other window. There I had an uninterrupted view of twelve miles of open landscape, with Mount Agamenticus in the purple distance. Not a house or a spire in sight. "Well," I exclaimed, "Greenton does n't appear to be a very closely packed metropolis!" That rival hotel with which I had threatened Mr. Sewell overnight was not a deadly weapon, looking at it by daylight. "By Jove!" I reflected, "maybe I'm in the wrong place." But there, tacked against a panel of the bedroom door, was a faded time-table dated Greenton, August 1, 1839.

I smiled all the time I was dressing, and went smiling down stairs, where I found Mr. Sewell, assisted by one of the fair sex in the first bloom of her eightieth year, serving breakfast for me on a small table—in the bar-room!

"I overslept myself this morning," I remarked apologetically, "and I see that I am putting you to some trouble. In future, if you will have me called, I will take my meals at the usual *table-d'hôte*."

"At the what?" said Mr. Sewell.

"I mean with the other boarders."

Mr. Sewell paused in the act of lifting a chop from the fire, and, resting the point of his fork against the woodwork of the mantel-piece, grinned from ear to ear.

"Bless you! there is n't any other boarders. There has n't been anybody put up here sence—let me see—sence father-in-law died, and that was in the fall of '40. To be sure, there's Silas; *he*'s a regular boarder; but I don't count him."

Mr. Sewell then explained how the tavern had lost its custom when the old stage line was broken up by the railroad. The introduction of steam was, in Mr. Sewell's estimation, a fatal error. "Jest killed local business. Carried it off I 'm darned if I know where. The whole country has been sort o' retrograding ever sence steam was invented."

"You spoke of having one boarder," I said.

"Silas? Yes; he came here the summer 'Tilda died,—she that was 'Tilda Bayley,—and he's here yet, going on thirteen year. He could n't live any longer with the old man. Between you and I, old Clem Jaffrey, Silas's father, was a hard nut. Yes," said Mr. Sewell, crooking his elbow in inimitable pantomime, "altogether too often. Found dead in the road hugging a three-gallon demijohn. *Habeas corpus* in the barn," added Mr. Sewell, intending, I presume, to intimate that a *post-mortem* examination had been deemed necessary. "Silas," he resumed, in that respectful tone which one should always adopt when speaking of capital, "is a man of considerable property; lives on his interest, and keeps a hoss and shay. He's a great scholar, too, Silas; takes all the pe-ri-odicals and the Police Gazette regular."

Mr. Sewell was turning over a third chop, when the door opened and a stoutish, middle-aged little gentleman, clad in deep black, stepped into the room.

"Silas Jaffrey," said Mr. Sewell, with a comprehensive sweep of his arm, picking up me and the newcomer on one fork, so to speak. "Be acquainted!"

Mr. Jaffrey advanced briskly, and gave me his hand with unlooked-for cordiality. He was a dapper little man, with a head as round and nearly as bald as an orange, and not unlike an orange in complexion, either; he had twinkling gray eyes and a pronounced Roman nose, the numerous freckles upon which were deepened by his funereal dress-coat and trousers. He reminded me of Alfred de Musset's blackbird, which, with its yellow beak and sombre plumage, looked like an undertaker eating an omelet.

"Silas will take care of yon," said Mr. Sewell, taking down his hat from a peg behind the door. "I 've got the cattle to look after. Tell him, if you want anything."

While I ate my breakfast, Mr. Jaffrey hopped up and down the narrow bar-room and chirped away as blithely as a bird on a cherry-bough, occasionally ruffling with his fingers a slight fringe of auburn hair which stood up pertly round his head and seemed to possess a luminous quality of its own.

"Don't I find it a little slow up here at the Corners? Not at all, my dear sir. I am in the thick of life up here. So many interesting things going on all over the world,—inventions, discoveries, spirits, railroad disasters, mysterious homicides. Poets, murderers, musicians, statesmen, distinguished travellers, prodigies of all kinds turning up everywhere. Very few events or persons escape me. I take six daily city papers, thirteen weekly journals, all the monthly magazines, and two quarterlies. I could not get along with less. I could n't if you asked me. I never feel lonely. How can I, being on intimate terms, as it were, with thousands and thousands of people? There 's that young woman out West. What an entertaining creature *she* is!—now in Missouri, now in Indiana, and now in Minnesota, always on the go, and all the time shedding needles from various parts of her body as if she really enjoyed it! Then there 's that versatile patriarch who walks hundreds of miles and saws thousands of feet of wood, before breakfast, and shows no signs of giving out. Then there 's that remarkable, one may say that historical colored woman who knew Benjamin Franklin, and fought at the battle of Bunk—no, it is the old negro man who fought at Bunker Hill, a mere infant, of course, at that period. Really, now, it is quite curious to observe how that venerable female slave—formerly an African princess—is repeatedly dying in her hundred and eleventh year, and coming to life again punctually every six months in the small-type paragraphs. Are you aware, sir, that within the last twelve years no fewer than two hundred and eighty-seven of General Washington's colored coachmen have died?"

For the soul of me I could n't tell whether this quaint little gentleman was chaffing me or not. I laid down my knife and fork, and stared at him.

"Then there are the mathematicians!" he cried vivaciously, without waiting for a reply. "I take great interest in them. Hear this!" and Mr. Jaffrey drew a newspaper from a pocket in the tail of his coat, and read as follows: "*It has been estimated that if all the candles manufactured by this eminent firm (Stearine & Co.) were placed end to end, they would reach 2 and ⅞ times around the globe.* Of course," continued Mr. Jaffrey, folding up the journal reflectively, "abstruse calculations of this kind are not, perhaps, of vital importance, but they indicate the intellectual activity of the age. Seriously, now," he said, halting in front of the table, "what with books and papers and drives about the country, I do not find the days too long, though I seldom see any one, except when I go over to K—— for my mail. Existence may be very full to a man who stands a little aside from the tumult and watches it with philosophic eye. Possibly he may see more of the battle than those who are in the midst of the action. Once I was struggling with the crowd, as eager and undaunted as the best; perhaps I should have been struggling still. Indeed, I know my life would have been very different now if I had married Mehetabel,—if I had married Mehetabel."

His vivacity was gone, a sudden cloud had come over his bright face, his figure seemed to have collapsed, the light seemed to have faded out of his hair. With a shuffling step, the very antithesis of his brisk, elastic tread, he turned to the door and passed into the road.

"Well," I said to myself, "if Greenton had forty thousand inhabitants, it could n't turn out a more astonishing old party than that!"

II
THE CASE OF SILAS JAFFREY

A man with a passion for *bric-à-brac* is always stumbling over antique bronzes, intaglios, mosaics, and daggers of the time of Benvenuto Cellini; the bibliophile finds creamy vellum folios and rare Alduses and Elzevirs waiting for him at unsuspected bookstalls; the numismatist has but to stretch forth his palm to have priceless coins drop into it. My own weakness is odd people, and I am constantly encountering them. It was plain I had unearthed a couple of very queer specimens at Bayley's Four-Corners. I saw that a fortnight afforded me too brief an opportunity to develop the richness of both, and I resolved to devote my spare time to Mr. Jaffrey alone, instinctively recognizing in him an unfamiliar species. My professional work in the vicinity of Greenton left my evenings and occasionally an afternoon unoccupied; these intervals I purposed to employ in studying and. classifying my fellow-boarder. It was necessary, as a preliminary step, to learn something of his previous history, and to this end I addressed myself to Mr. Sewell that same night.

"I do not want to seem inquisitive," I said to the landlord, as he was fastening up the bar, which, by the way, was the *salle à manger* and general sitting-room,—"I do not want to seem inquisitive, but your friend Mr. Jaffrey dropped a remark this morning at breakfast which—which was not altogether dear to me."

"About Mehetabel?" asked Mr. Sewell, uneasily.

"Yes."

"Well, I wish he would n't!"

"He was friendly enough in the course of conversation to hint to me that he had not married the young woman, and seemed to regret it."

"No, he did n't marry Mehetabel."

"May I inquire *why* he did n't marry Mehetabel?"

"Never asked her. Might have married the girl forty times. Old Elkins's daughter, over at K——. She 'd have had him quick enough. Seven years, off and on, he kept company with Mehetabel, and then she died."

"And he never asked her? "

"He shilly-shallied. Perhaps he did n't think of it. When she was dead and gone, then Silas was struck all of a heap,—and that 's all about it."

Obviously Mr. Sewell did not intend to tell me anything more, and obviously there was more to tell. The topic was plainly disagreeable to him for some reason or other, and that unknown reason of course piqued my curiosity.

As I was absent from dinner and supper that day, I did not meet Mr. Jaffrey again until the following morning at breakfast. He had recovered his bird-like manner, and was full of a mysterious assassination that had just taken place in New York, all the thrilling details of which were at his fingers' ends. It was at once comical and sad to see this harmless old gentleman, with his naïve, benevolent countenance, and his thin hair flaming up in a semicircle, like the foot-lights at a theatre, revelling in the intricacies of the unmentionable deed.

"You come up to my room to-night," he cried, with horrid glee, "and I 'll give you my theory of the murder. I 'll make it as clear as day to you that it was the detective himself who fired the three pistol-shots."

It was not so much the desire to have this point elucidated as to make a closer study of Mr. Jaffrey that led me to accept his invitation. Mr. Jaffrey's bedroom was in an L of the building, and was in no way noticeable except for the numerous files of newspapers neatly arranged against the blank spaces of the walls, and a huge pile of old magazines which stood in one corner, reaching nearly up to the ceiling, and threatening to topple over each instant, like the Leaning Tower at Pisa. There were green paper shades at the windows, some faded chintz valances about the bed, and two or three easy-chairs covered with chintz. On a black-walnut shelf between the windows lay a choice collection of meerschaum and brierwood pipes.

Filling one of the chocolate-colored bowls for me and another for himself, Mr. Jaffrey began prattling; but not about the murder, which appeared to have flown out of his mind. In fact, I do not remember that the topic was even touched upon, either then or afterwards.

"Cosey nest this," said Mr. Jaffrey, glancing complacently over the apartment. "What is more cheerful, now, in the fall of the year, than an open wood-fire? Do you hear those little chirps and twitters coming out of that piece of apple-wood? Those are the ghosts of the robins and bluebirds that sang upon the bough when it was in blossom last spring. In summer whole flocks of them come fluttering about the fruit-trees under the window: so I have singing birds all the year round. I take it very easy here, I can tell you, summer and winter. Not much society. Tobias is not, perhaps, what one would term a great intellectual force, but he means well. He 's a realist,—believes in coming down to what he calls 'the hard pan'; but his heart is in the right place, and he's very kind to me. The wisest thing I ever did in my life was to sell out my grain business over at K——, thirteen years ago, and settle down at the Corners. When a man has made a competency, what does he want more? Besides, at that time an event occurred which destroyed any ambition I may have had. Mehetabel died."

"The lady you were engaged to?"

"N-o, not precisely engaged. I think it was quite understood between us, though nothing had been said on the subject. Typhoid," added Mr. Jaffrey, in a low voice.

For several minutes he smoked in silence, a vague, troubled look playing over his countenance. Presently this passed away, and he fixed his gray eyes speculatively upon my face.

"If I had married Mehetabel," said Mr. Jaffrey, slowly, and then he hesitated. I blew a ring of smoke into the air, and, resting my pipe on my knee, dropped into an attitude of attention. "If I had married Mehetabel, you know, we should have had—ahem!—a family."

"Very likely," I assented, vastly amused at this unexpected turn.

"A Boy!" exclaimed Mr. Jaffrey, explosively.

"By all means, certainly, a son."

"Great trouble about naming the boy. Mehetabel's family want him named Elkanah Elkins, after her grandfather; I want him named Andrew Jackson. We compromise by christening him Elkanah Elkins Andrew Jackson Jaffrey. Rather a long name for such a short little fellow," said Mr. Jaffrey, musingly.

"Andy is n't a bad nickname," I suggested.

"Not at all. We call him Andy, in the family. Somewhat fractious at first,—colic and things. I suppose it is right, or it would n't be so; but the usefulness of measles, mumps, croup, whooping-cough, scarlatina, and fits is not visible to the naked eye. I wish Andy would be a model infant, and dodge the whole lot."

This supposititious child, born within the last few minutes, was clearly assuming the proportions of a reality to Mr. Jaffrey. I began to feel a little uncomfortable. I am, as I have said, a civil engineer, and it is not strictly in my line to assist at the births of infants, imaginary or otherwise. I pulled away vigorously at the pipe, and said nothing.

"What large blue eyes he has," resumed Mr. Jaffrey, after a pause; "just like Hetty's; and the fair hair, too, like hers. How oddly certain distinctive features are handed down in families! Sometimes a mouth, sometimes a turn of the eyebrow. Wicked little boys, over at K——, have now and then derisively advised me to follow my nose. It would be an interesting thing to do. I should find my nose flying about the world, turning up unexpectedly here and there, dodging this branch of the family and reappearing in that, now jumping over one great-grandchild to fasten itself upon another, and never losing its individuality. Look at Andy. There 's Elkanah Elkins's chin to the life. Andy's chin is probably older than the Pyramids. Poor little thing," he cried, with sudden indescribable tenderness, "to lose his mother so early!" And Mr. Jaffrey's head sunk upon his breast, and his shoulders slanted forward, as if he were actually bending over the cradle of the child. The whole gesture and attitude was so natural that it startled me. The pipe slipped from my fingers and fell to the floor.

"Hush!" whispered Mr. Jaffrey, with a deprecating motion of his hand. "Andy 's asleep!"

He rose softly from the chair and, walking across the room on tiptoe, drew down the shade at the window through which the moonlight was streaming. Then he returned to his seat, and remained gazing with half-closed eyes into the dropping embers.

I refilled my pipe and smoked in profound silence, wondering what would come next. But nothing came next. Mr. Jaffrey had fallen into so brown a study that, a quarter of an hour afterwards, when I wished him good night and withdrew, I do not think he noticed my departure.

I am not what is called a man of imagination; it is my habit to exclude most things not capable of mathematical demonstration; but I am not without a certain psychological insight, and I think I understood Mr. Jaffrey's case. I could easily understand how a man with an unhealthy, sensitive nature, overwhelmed by sudden calamity, might take refuge in some forlorn place like this old tavern, and dream his life away. To such a man—brooding forever on what might have been and dwelling wholly in the realm of his fancies—the actual world might indeed become as a dream, and nothing seem real but his illusions. I dare say that thirteen years of Bayley's Four-Corners would have its effect upon me; though instead of conjuring up golden-haired children of the Madonna, I should probably see gnomes and kobolds, and goblins engaged in hoisting false signals and misplacing switches for midnight express trains.

"No doubt," I said to myself that night, as I lay in bed, thinking over the matter, "this once possible but now impossible child is a great comfort to the old gentleman,—a greater comfort, perhaps, than a real son would be. May be Andy will vanish with the shades and mists of night, he 's such an unsubstantial infant; but if he does n't, and Mr. Jaffrey finds pleasure in talking to me about his son, I shall humor the old fellow. It would n't be a Christian act to knock over his harmless fancy."

I was very impatient to see if Mr. Jaffrey's illusion would stand the test of daylight. It did. Elkanah Elkins Andrew Jackson Jaffrey was, so to speak, alive and kicking the next morning. On taking his seat at the breakfast-table, Mr. Jaffrey whispered to me that Andy had had a comfortable night.

"Silas!" said Mr. Sewell, sharply, "what are you whispering about? "

Mr. Sewell was in an ill-humor; perhaps he was jealous because I had passed the evening in Mr. Jaffrey's room; but surely Mr. Sewell could not expect his boarders to go to bed at eight o'clock every night, as he did. From time to time during the meal Mr. Sewell regarded me unkindly out of the corner of his eye, and in helping me to the parsnips he poniarded them with quite a suggestive air. All this, however, did not prevent me from repairing to the door of Mr. Jaffrey's snuggery when night came.

"Well, Mr. Jaffrey, how 's Andy this evening?"

"Got a tooth!" cried Mr. Jaffrey, vivaciously.

"No!"

"Yes, he has! Just through. Gave the nurse a silver dollar. Standing reward for first tooth."

It was on the tip of my tongue to express surprise that an infant a day old should cut a tooth, when I suddenly recollected that Richard III was born with teeth. Feeling myself to be on unfamiliar ground, I suppressed my criticism. It was well I did so, for in the next breath I was advised that half a year had elapsed since the previous evening.

"Andy's had a hard six months of it," said Mr. Jaffrey, with the well-known narrative air of fathers. "We 've brought him up by hand. His grandfather, by the way, was brought up by the bottle"—and brought down by it, too, I added mentally, recalling Mr. Sewell's account of the old gentleman's tragic end.

Mr. Jaffrey then went on to give me a history of Andy's first six months, omitting no detail however insignificant or irrelevant. This history I would, in turn, inflict upon the reader, if I were only certain that he is one of those dreadful parents who, under the ægis of friendship, bore you at a street-corner with that remarkable thing which Freddy said the other day, and insist on singing to you, at an evening party, the Iliad of Tommy's woes.

But to inflict this *enfantillage* upon the unmarried reader would be an act of wanton cruelty. So I pass over that part of Andy's biography, and, for the same reason, make no record of the next four or five interviews I had with Mr. Jaffrey. It will be sufficient to state that Andy glided from extreme infancy to early youth with astonishing celerity,—at the rate of one year per night, if I remember correctly; and—must I confess it?—before the week came to an end, this invisible hobgoblin of a boy was only little less of a reality to me than to Mr. Jaffrey.

At first I had lent myself to the old dreamer's whim with a keen perception of the humor of the thing; but by and by I found I was talking and thinking of Miss Mehetabel's son as though he were a veritable personage. Mr. Jaffrey spoke of the child with such an air of conviction!—as if Andy were playing among his toys in the next room, or making mud-pies down in the yard. In these conversations, it should be observed, the child was never supposed to be present, except on that single occasion when Mr. Jaffrey leaned over the cradle. After one of our *séances* I would lie awake until the small hours, thinking of the boy, and then fall asleep only to have indigestible dreams about him. Through the day, and sometimes in the midst of complicated calculations, I would catch myself wondering what Andy was up to now! There was no shaking him off; he became an inseparable nightmare to me; and I felt that if I remained much longer at Bayley's Four-Corners I should turn into just such another bald-headed, mild-eyed visionary as Silas Jaffrey.

Then the tavern was a grewsome old shell any way, full of unaccountable noises after dark,— rustlings of garments along unfrequented passages, and stealthy footfalls in unoccupied chambers overhead. I never knew of an old house without these mysterious noises. Next to my bedroom was a musty, dismantled apartment, in one corner of which, leaning against the wainscot, was a crippled mangle, with its iron crank tilted in the air like the elbow of the late Mr. Clem Jaffrey. Sometimes,

"In the dead vast and middle of the night,"

I used to hear sounds as if some one were turning that rusty crank on the sly. This occurred only on particularly cold nights, and I conceived the uncomfortable idea that it was the thin family ghosts, from the neglected graveyard in the cornfield, keeping themselves warm by running each other through the mangle. There was a haunted air about the whole place that made it easy for me to believe in the existence of a phantasm like Miss Mehetabel's son, who, after all, was less unearthly than Mr. Jaffrey himself, and seemed more properly an inhabitant of this globe than the toothless ogre who kept the inn, not to mention the silent Witch of Endor that cooked our meals for us over the bar-room fire.

In spite of the scowls and winks bestowed upon me by Mr. Sewell, who let slip no opportunity to testify his disapprobation of the intimacy, Mr. Jaffrey and I spent all our evenings together,—those long autumnal evenings, through the length of which he talked about the boy, laying out his path in life and hedging the path with roses. He should be sent to the High School at Portsmouth, and then to college; he should be educated like a gentleman, Andy.

"When the old man dies," said Mr. Jaffrey, rubbing his hands gleefully, as if it were a great joke, "Andy will find that the old man has left him a pretty plum."

"What do you think of having Andy enter West Point, when he 's old enough?" said Mr. Jaffrey on another occasion. "He need n't necessarily go into the army when he graduates; he can become a civil engineer."

This was a stroke of flattery so delicate and indirect that I could accept it without immodesty.

There had lately sprung up on the corner of Mr. Jaffrey's bureau a small tin house, Gothic in architecture, and pink in color, with a slit in the roof, and the word BANK painted on one façade. Several times in the course of an evening Mr. Jaffrey would rise from his chair without interrupting the conversation, and gravely drop a nickel into the scuttle of the bank. It was pleasant to observe the solemnity of his countenance as he approached the edifice, and the air of triumph with which he resumed his seat by the fireplace. One night I missed the tin bank. It had disappeared, deposits and all. Evidently there had been a defalcation on rather a large scale. I strongly suspected that Mr. Sewell was at the bottom of it; but my suspicion was not shared by Mr. Jaffrey, who, remarking my glance at the bureau, became suddenly depressed. "I 'm afraid," he said, "that I have failed to instil into Andrew those principles of integrity which—which—" and the old gentleman quite broke down.

Andy was now eight or nine years old, and for some time past, if the truth most be told, had given Mr. Jaffrey no inconsiderable trouble; what with his impishness and his illnesses, the boy led the pair of us a lively dance. I shall not soon forget the anxiety of Mr. Jaffrey the night Andy had the scarlet-fever,—an anxiety which so infected me that I actually returned to the tavern the following afternoon earlier than usual, dreading to hear the little spectre was dead, and greatly relieved on meeting Mr. Jaffrey at the door-step with his face wreathed in smiles. When I spoke to him of Andy, I was made aware that I was inquiring into a case of scarlet-fever that had occurred the year before!

It was at this time, towards the end of my second week at Greenton, that I noticed what was probably not a new trait,—Mr. Jaffrey's curious sensitiveness to atmospherical changes. He was as sensitive as a barometer. The approach of a storm sent his mercury down instantly. When the weather was fair, he was hopeful and sunny, and Andy's prospects were brilliant. When the weather was overcast and threatening, he grew restless and despondent, and was afraid the boy was n't going to turn out well.

On the Saturday previous to my departure, which had been fixed for Monday, it rained heavily all the afternoon, and that night Mr. Jaffrey was in an unusually excitable and unhappy frame of mind. His mercury was very low indeed.

"That boy is going to the dogs just as fast as he can go," said Mr. Jaffrey, with a woful face. "I can't do anything with him."

"He 'll come out all right, Mr. Jaffrey. Boys will be boys. I would not give a snap for a lad without animal spirits."

"But animal spirits," said Mr. Jaffrey sententiously, "should n't saw off the legs of the piano in Tobias's best parlor. I don't know what Tobias will say when he finds it out."

"What! has Andy sawed off the legs of the old spinet?" I returned, laughing.

"Worse than that."

"Played upon it, then!"

"No, sir. He has lied to me!"

"I can't believe that of Andy."

"Lied to me, sir," repeated Mr. Jaffrey, severely. "He pledged me his word of honor that he would give over his climbing. The way that boy climbs sends a chill down my spine. This morning, not-withstanding his solemn promise, he shinned up the lightning-rod attached to the extension and sat astride the ridge-pole. I saw him, and he denied it! When a boy you have caressed and indulged, and lavished pocket-money on, lies to you and *will* climb, then there 's nothing more to be said. He 's a lost child."

"You take too dark a view of it, Mr. Jaffrey. Train-ing and education are bound to tell in the end, and he has been well brought up."

"But I did n't bring him up on a lightning-rod, did I? If he is ever going to know how to behave, he ought to know now. To-morrow he will be eleven years old."

The reflection came to me that if Andy had not been brought up by the rod, he had certainly been brought up by the lightning. He was eleven years old in two weeks!

I essayed, with that perspicacious wisdom which seems to be the peculiar property of bachelors and elderly maiden ladies, to tranquillize Mr. Jaffrey's mind, and to give him some practical hints on the management of youth.

"Spank him," I suggested at length.

"I will!" said the old gentleman.

"And you 'd better do it at once!" I added, as it flashed upon me that in six months Andy would be a hundred and forty-three years old!—an age at which parental discipline would have to be relaxed.

The next morning, Sunday, the rain came down as if determined to drive the quicksilver entirely out of my poor friend. Mr. Jaffrey sat bolt upright at the breakfast-table, looking as woe-begone as a bust of Dante, and retired to his chamber the moment the meal was finished. As the day advanced, the wind veered round to the northeast, and settled itself down to work. It was not pleasant to think, and I tried not to think, what Mr. Jaffrey's condition would be if the weather did not mend its manners by noon; but so far from clearing off at noon, the storm increased in violence, and as night set in, the wind whistled in a spiteful falsetto key, and the rain lashed the old tavern as if it were a balky horse that refused to move on. The windows rattled in the worm-eaten frames, and the doors of remote rooms, where nobody ever went, slammed to in the maddest way. Now and then the tornado, sweeping down the side of Mount Agamenticus, bowled across the open country, and struck the ancient hostelry point-blank.

Mr. Jaffrey did not appear at supper. I knew he was expecting me to come to his room as usual, and I turned over in my mind a dozen plans to evade

seeing him that night. The landlord sat at the opposite side of the chimney-place, with his eye upon
me. I fancy he was aware of the effect of this storm
on his other boarder, for at intervals, as the wind
hurled itself against the exposed gable, threatening
to burst in the windows, Mr. Sewell tipped me an
atrocious wink, and displayed his gums in a way he
had not done since the morning after my arrival at
Greenton. I wondered if he suspected anything about
Andy. There had been odd times during the past
week when I felt convinced that the existence of
Miss Mehetabel's son was no secret to Mr. Sewell.

In deference to the gale, the landlord sat up half
an hour later than was his custom. At half past eight
he went to bed, remarking that he thought the old
pile would stand till morning.

He had been absent only a few minutes when I
heard a rustling at the door. I looked up, and beheld
Mr. Jaffrey standing on the threshold, with his dress
in disorder, his scant hair flying, and the wildest
expression on his face.

"He 's gone!" cried Mr. Jaffrey.

"Who? Sewell? Yes, he just went to bed."

"No, not Tobias,—the boy! "

"What, run away?"

"No,—he is dead! He has fallen off of a step-
ladder in the red chamber and broken his neck!"

Mr. Jaffrey threw up his hands with a gesture of
despair, and disappeared. I followed him through

the hall, saw him go into his own apartment, and heard the bolt of the door drawn to. Then I returned to the bar-room, and sat for an hour or two in the ruddy glow of the fire, brooding over the strange experience of the last fortnight.

On my way to bed I paused at Mr. Jaffrey's door, and, in a lull of the storm, the measured respiration within told me that the old gentleman was sleeping peacefully.

Slumber was coy with me that night. I lay listening to the soughing of the wind, and thinking of Mr. Jaffrey's illusion. It had amused me at first with its grotesqueness; but now the poor little phantom was dead, I was conscious that there had been something pathetic in it all along. Shortly after midnight the wind sunk down, coming and going fainter and fainter, floating around the eaves of the tavern with a gentle, murmurous sound, as if it were turning itself into soft wings to bear away the spirit of a little child.

Perhaps nothing that happened during my stay at Bayley's Four-Corners took me so completely by surprise as Mr. Jaffrey's radiant countenance the next morning. The morning itself was not fresher or sunnier. His round face literally shone with geniality and happiness. His eyes twinkled like diamonds, and the magnetic light of his hair was turned on full. He came into my room while I was packing my valise. He chirped, and prattled, and carolled, and was sorry I was going away,—but never a word about Andy. However, the boy had probably been dead several years then!

The open wagon that was to carry me to the station stood at the door; Mr. Sewell was placing my case of instruments under the seat, and Mr. Jaffrey had gone up to his room to get me a certain newspaper containing an account of a remarkable shipwreck on the Auckland Islands. I took the opportunity to thank Mr. Sewell for his courtesies to me, and to express my regret at leaving him and Mr. Jaffrey.

"I have become very much attached to Mr. Jaffrey," I said; "he is a most interesting person; but that hypothetical boy of his, that son of Miss Mehetabel's—"

"Yes, I know!" interrupted Mr. Sewell, testily. "Fell off a step-ladder and broke his dratted neck. Eleven year old, was n't he? Always does, jest at that point. Next week Silas will begin the whole thing over again, if he can get anybody to listen to him."

"I see. Our amiable friend is a little queer on that subject."

Mr. Sewell glanced cautiously over his shoulder, and, tapping himself significantly on the forehead, said in a low voice,

"Room To Let—Unfurnished!"

Fire-Worship

[NATHANIEL HAWTHORNE]

It is a great revolution in social and domestic life—and no less so in the life of the secluded student—this almost universal exchange of the open fire-place for the cheerless and ungenial stove. On such a morning as now lowers around our old gray parsonage I miss the bright face of my ancient friend who was wont to dance upon the hearth and play the part of a more familiar sunshine. It is sad to turn from the cloudy sky and somber landscape— from yonder hill with its crown of rusty black pines, the foliage of which is so dismal in the absence of the sun; that bleak pasture-land and the broken surface of the potato field with the brown clods partly concealed by the snowfall of last night; the swollen and sluggish river, with ice-incrusted borders, dragging its bluish-gray stream along the verge of our orchard like a snake half torpid with the cold—it is sad to turn from an outward scene of so little comfort and find the same sullen influences brooding within the precincts of my study. Where is that brilliant guest, that quick and subtle spirit whom Prometheus lured from heaven to civilize mankind and cheer them in their wintry desolation, that comfortable inmate whose smile during eight months of the year was our sufficient consolation for summer's lingering advance and early flight? Alas! blindly inhospitable, grudging the food that kept him cheery and mercurial, we have thrust him into an iron prison and compel him to smolder away his life on a daily pittance which once would have been too scanty for his breakfast. Without a metaphor, we now make our fire in the air-tight stove and supply it with some half a dozen sticks of wood between dawn and nightfall.

I never shall be reconciled to this enormity. Truly may it be said that the world looks darker for it. In one way or another, here and there and all around us, the inventions of mankind are fast blotting the picturesque, the poetic and the beautiful out of human life. The domestic fire was a type of all these attributes, and seemed to bring might and majesty and wild Nature and a spiritual essence into our inmost home, and yet to dwell with us in such friendliness that its mysteries and marvels excited no dismay. The same mild companion that smiled so placidly in our faces was he that comes roaring out of Ætna and rushes madly up the sky like a fiend breaking loose from torment and fighting for a place among the upper angels. He it is, too, that leaps from cloud to cloud amid the crashing thunderstorm. It was he whom the Gheber worshiped with no unnatural idolatry, and it was he who devoured London and Moscow, and many another famous city, and who loves to riot through our dark forests and sweep across our prairies, and to whose ravenous maw, it is said, the universe shall one day be given as a final feast. Meanwhile, he is the great artisan and laborer by whose aid men are enabled to build a world within a world—or, at least, to smooth down the rough creation which Nature flung to us. He forges the mighty anchor and every lesser instrument, he drives the steamboat and drags the rail-car, and it was he—this creature of terrible might and so many-sided utility and all-comprehensive destructiveness—that used to be the cheerful, homely friend of our wintry days, and whom we have made the prisoner of this iron cage.

How kindly he was, and, though the tremendous agent of change, yet bearing himself with such gentleness, so rendering himself a part of all life-long and age-coeval associations, that it seemed as if he were the great conservative of Nature. While a man was true to the fireside, so long would he be true to country and law, to the God whom his fathers worshiped, to the wife of his youth, and to all things else which instinct or religion have taught us to consider sacred. With how sweet humility did this elemental spirit perform all needful offices for the household in which he was domesticated! He was equal to the concoction of a grand dinner, yet scorned not to roast a potato or toast a bit of cheese. How humanely did he cherish the school-boy's icy fingers and thaw the old man's joints with a genial warmth which almost equaled the glow of youth! And how carefully did he dry the cowhide boots that had trudged through mud and snow, and the shaggy outside garment stiff with frozen sleet, taking heed, likewise, to the comfort of the faithful dog who had followed his master through the storm! When did he refuse a coal to light a pipe, or even a part of his own substance to kindle a neigh-bor's fire? And then, at twilight, when laborer or scholar, or mortal of whatever age, sex or degree, drew a chair beside him and looked into his glow-ing face, how acute, how profound, how compre-hensive, was his sympathy with the mood of each and all! He pictured forth their very thoughts. To the youthful he showed the scenes of the adventur-ous life before them; to the aged, the shadows of departed love and hope; and if all earthly things had grown distasteful, he could gladden the fireside-muser with golden glimpses of a better world. And amid this varied communion with the human soul how busily would the sympathizer, the deep moralist, the painter of magic pictures, be causing the tea-kettle to boil!

Nor did it lessen the charm of his soft, familiar courtesy and helpfulness that the mighty spirit, were opportunity offered him, would run riot through the peaceful house, wrap its inmates in his terrible embrace, and leave nothing to them save their whitened bones. This possibility of mad destruction only made his domestic kindness the more beautiful and touching. It was so sweet of him, being endowed with such power, to dwell day after day, and one long, lonesome night after another, on the dusky hearth, only now and then betraying his wild nature by thrusting his red tongue out of the chimney-top! True, he had done much mischief in the world, and was pretty certain to do more, but his warm heart atoned for all. He was kindly to the race of man, and they pardoned his characteristic imperfections.

The good old clergyman, my predecessor in this mansion, was well acquainted with the comforts of the fireside. His yearly allowance of wood, according to the terms of his settlement, was no less than sixty cords. Almost an annual forest was converted from sound oak-logs into ashes in the kitchen, the parlor, and this little study where now an unworthy successor—not in the pastoral office, but merely in his earthly abode—sits scribbling beside an air-tight stove. I love to fancy one of those fireside days while the good man, a contemporary of the Revolution, was in his early prime, some sixty-five years ago. Before sunrise, doubtless, the blaze hovered upon the gray skirts of night and dissolved the frost-work that had gathered like a curtain over the small window-panes. There is something peculiar in the aspect of the morning fireside—a fresher, brisker glare, the absence of that mellowness which can be produced only by half-consumed logs and shapeless brands with the white ashes on them and mighty coals, the remnant of tree-trunks that the hungry elements have gnawed for hours. The morning hearth, too, is newly swept and the brazen andirons well brightened; so that the cheerful fire may see its face in them. Surely it was happiness when the pastor, fortified with a substantial breakfast, sat down in his arm-chair and slippers and opened the "Whole Body of Divinity" or the "Commentary on Job," or whichever of his old folios or quartos might fall within the range of his weekly sermons. It must have been his own fault if the warmth and glow of this abundant hearth did not permeate the discourse and keep his audience comfortable in spite of the bitterest northern blast that ever wrestled with the church-steeple. He reads while the heat warps the stiff covers of the volume, he writes without numbness either in his heart or fingers, and with unstinted hand he throws fresh sticks of wood upon the fire.

A parishioner comes in. With what warmth of benevolence—how should he be otherwise than warm in any of his attributes?—does the minister bid him welcome and set a chair for him in so close proximity to the hearth that soon the guest finds it needful to rub his scorched shins with his great red hands? The melted snow drips from his steaming boots and bubbles upon the hearth. His puckered forehead unravels its entanglement of criss-cross wrinkles. We lose much of the enjoyment of fire-side heat without such an opportunity of marking its genial effect upon those who have been looking the inclement weather in the face. In the course of the day our clergyman himself strides forth, per-chance to pay a round of pastoral visits, or, it may be, to visit his mountain of a wood-pile and cleave the monstrous logs into billets suitable for the fire. He returns with fresher life to his beloved hearth. During the short afternoon the western sunshine comes into the study and strives to stare the ruddy blaze out of countenance, but with only a brief triumph, soon to be succeeded by brighter glories of its rival. Beautiful it is to see the strengthening gleam, the deepening light, that gradually casts distinct shadows of the human figure, the table and the high-backed chairs upon the opposite wall, and at length, as twilight comes on, replenishes the room with living radiance and makes life all rose-color. Afar the wayfarer discerns the flickering flame as it dances upon the windows, and hails it as a beacon-light of humanity, reminding him, in his cold and lonely path, that the world is not all snow and solitude and desolation. At eventide, probably, the study was peopled with the clergyman's wife and family, and children tumbled themselves upon the hearth-rug, and grave Puss sat with her back to the fire or gazed with a semblance of human meditation into its fervid depths. Seasonably the plenteous ashes of the day were raked over the moldering brands, and from the heap came jets of flame and an incense of night-long smoke creeping quietly up the chimney.

Heaven forgive the old clergyman! In his later life, when for almost ninety winters he had been gladdened by the firelight—when it had gleamed upon him from infancy to extreme age, and never without brightening his spirits as well as his visage, and perhaps keeping him alive so long—he had the heart to brick up his chimney-place and bid farewell to the face of his old friend forever. Why did not he take an eternal leave of the sunshine, too? His sixty cords of wood had probably dwindled to a far less ample supply in modern times, and it is certain that the parsonage had grown crazy with time and tempest and pervious to the cold; but still it was one of the saddest tokens of the decline and fall of open fire-places that the gray patriarch should have deigned to warm himself at an air-tight stove.

And I, likewise, who have found a home in this ancient owl's nest since its former occupant took his heavenward flight—I, to my shame, have put up stoves in kitchen and parlor and chamber. Wander where you will about the house, not a glimpse of the earth-born, heaven-aspiring fiend of Ætna—him that sports in the thunderstorm, the idol of the Ghebers, the devourer of cities, the forest-rioter and prairie-sweeper, the future destroyer of our earth, the old chimney-corner companion who mingles himself so sociably with household joys and sorrows—not a glimpse of this mighty and kindly one will greet your eyes. He is now an invisible presence. There is his iron cage; touch it and he scorches your fingers. He delights to singe a garment or perpetrate any other little unworthy mischief, for his temper is ruined by the ingratitude of mankind, for whom he cherished such a warmth of feeling, and to whom he taught all their arts, even that of making his own prison-house. In his fits of rage he puffs volumes of smoke and noisome gas through the crevices of the door and shakes the iron walls of his dungeon so as to overthrow the ornamental urn upon its summit. We tremble lest he should break forth among us. Much of his time is spent in sighs burdened with unutterable grief and long drawn through the funnel. He amuses himself, too, with repeating all the whispers, the moans and the louder utterances or tempestuous howls of the wind; so that the stove becomes a microcosm of the aerial world. Occasionally there, are strange combinations of sounds—voices talking almost articulately within the hollow chest of iron—insomuch that Fancy beguiles me with the idea that my fire-wood must have grown in that infernal forest of lamentable trees which breathed their complaints to Dante. When the listener is half-asleep he may readily take these voices for the conversation of spirits and assign them an intelligible meaning. Anon, there is a pattering noise—drip, drip, drip—as if a summer shower was falling within the narrow circumference of the stove.

These barren and tedious eccentricities are all that the air-tight stove can bestow in exchange for the invaluable moral influences which we have lost by our desertion of the open fire-place. Alas! is this world so very bright that we can afford to choke up such a domestic fountain of gladsomeness and sit down by its darkened source without being conscious of a gloom?

It is my belief that social intercouse cannot long continue what it has been now that we have subtracted from it so important and vivifying an element as firelight. The effects will be more perceptible on our children and the generations that shall succeed them than on ourselves, the mechanism of whose life may remain unchanged, though its spirit be far other than it was. The sacred trust of the household fire has been transmitted in unbroken succession from the earliest ages and faithfully cherished in spite of every discouragement, such as the curfew law of the Norman conquerors, until in these evil days physical science has nearly succeeded in extinguishing it. But we, at least, have our youthful recollections tinged with the glow of the hearth and our lifelong habits and associations arranged on the principle of a mutual bond in the domestic fire. Therefore, though the sociable friend be forever departed, yet in a degree he will be spiritually present with us and still more will the empty forms which were once full of his rejoicing presence continue to rule our manners. We shall draw our chairs together as we and our forefathers have been wont for thousands of years back and sit around some blank and empty corner of the room babbling with unreal cheerfulness of topics suitable to the homely fireside. A warmth from the past—from the ashes of bygone years and the raked-up embers of long ago—will sometimes thaw the ice about our hearts. But it must be otherwise with our successors. On the most favorable supposition, they will be acquainted with the fireside in no better shape than that of the sullen stove, and more probably they will have grown up amid furnace-heat in houses which might be fancied to have their foundation over the infernal pit whence sulphurous steams and unbreathable exhalations ascend through the apertures of the floor. There will be nothing to attract these poor children to one center. They will never behold one another through that peculiar medium of vision—the ruddy gleam of blazing wood or bituminous coal—which gives the human spirit so deep an insight into its fellows and melts all humanity into one cordial heart of hearts. Domestic life—if it may still be termed domestic—will seek its separate corners and never gather itself into groups. The easy gossip, the merry yet unambitious jest, the lifelike practical discussion of real matters in a casual way, the soul of truth which is so often incarnated in a simple fireside word, will disappear from earth. Conversation will contract the air of a debate and all mortal intercourse be chilled with a fatal frost.

In classic times the exhortation to fight *pro aris et focis*—"for the altars and the hearths"—was considered the strongest appeal that could be made to patriotism. And it seemed an immortal utterance, for all subsequent ages and people have acknowledged its force and responded to it with the full portion of manhood that nature had assigned to each. Wisely were the altar and the hearth conjoined in one mighty sentence, for the hearth, too, had its kindred sanctity. Religion sat down beside it—not in the priestly robes which decorated and perhaps disguised her at the altar, but arrayed in a simple matron's garb and uttering her lessons with the tenderness of a mother's voice and heart. The holy hearth! If any earthly and material thing—or, rather, a divine idea embodied in brick and mortar—might be supposed to possess the permanence of moral truth, it was this. All revered it. The man who did not put off his shoes upon this holy ground would have deemed it pastime to trample upon the altar. It has been our task to uproot the hearth; what further reform is left for our children to achieve unless they overthrow the altar too? And by what appeal hereafter, when the breath of hostile armies may mingle with the pure cold breezes of our country, shall we attempt to rouse up native valor? Fight for your hearths? There will be none throughout the land. Fight for your stoves? Not I, in faith. If in such a cause I strike a blow it shall be on the invader's part, and heaven grant that it may shatter the abomination all to pieces!

Law Lane

[SARAH ORNE JEWETT]

I

The thump of a flat-iron signified to an educated passer-by that this was Tuesday morning; yesterday having been fair and the weekly washing-day unhindered by the weather. It was undoubtedly what Mrs. Powder pleased herself by calling a good orthodox week; not one of the disjointed and imperfect sections of time which a rainy Monday forced upon methodical housekeepers. Mrs. Powder was not a woman who could live altogether in the present, and whatever she did was done with a view to having it cleared out of the way of the next enterprise on her list. "I can't bear to see folks do their work as if every piece on 't was a treadmill," she used to say, briskly. "Life means progriss to me, and I can't dwell by the way no more 'n sparks can fly downwards. 'T ain't the way I'm built, nor none of the Fisher tribe."

The hard white bundles in the shallow splint-basket were disappearing, one by one, and taking their places on the decrepit clothes-horse, well ironed and precisely folded. The July sunshine came in at one side of Mrs. Powder's kitchen, and the cool northwest breeze blew the heat out again from the other side. Mrs. Powder grew uneasy and impatient as she neared the end of her task, and the flat-iron moved more and more vigorously. She kept glancing out through the doorway and along the country road as if she were watching for somebody.

"I shall just have to git ready an' go an' rout her out myself, an' take my chances," she said at last with a resentful look at the clock, as if it were partly to blame for the delay and had ears with which to listen to proper rebuke. The round moon-face had long ago ceased its waxing and waning across the upper part of the old dial, as if it had forgotten its responsibility about the movements of a heavenly body in its pleased concern about housekeeping.

"See here!" said Mrs. Powder, taking a last hot iron from the fire. "You ain't a-keepin' time like you used to; you're gettin' lazy, I must say. Look at this 'ere sun-mark on the floor, that calls it full 'leven o'clock, and you want six minutes to ten. I've got to send word to the clock-man and have your

in'ards all took apart; you got me to meetin' more 'n
half an hour too late, Sabbath last."

To which the moon-face did not change its beaming expression; very likely, being a moon, it was not
willing to mind the ways of the sun.

"Lord, what an old thing you be!" said Mrs. Powder, turning away with a chuckle. "I don't wonder
your sense kind of fails you!" And the clock clucked
at her by way of answer, though presently it was
going to strike ten at any rate.

The hot iron was now put down hurriedly, and
the half-ironed night-cap was left in a queer position on the ironing-board. A small figure had
appeared in the road and was coming toward the
house with a fleet, barefooted run which required
speedy action. "Here you, Joel Smith!" shouted the
old woman. "Jo—el!" But the saucy lad only doubled his pace and pretended not to see or hear her.
Mrs. Powder could play at that game, too, and did
not call again, but quietly went back to her ironing
and tried as hard as she could to be provoked.
Presently the boy came panting up the slope of green
turf which led from the road to the kitchen doorstep.

"I did n't know but you spoke as I ran by," he
remarked, in an amiable tone. Mrs. Powder took no
heed of him whatever.

"I ain't in no hurry; I kind o' got running." he
explained, a moment later; and then, as his hostess
stepped toward the stove, he caught up the frilled

night-cap and tied it on in a twinkling. When Mrs. Powder turned again, the sight of him was too much for her gravity.

"Them frills is real becoming to ye," she announced, shaking with laughter. "I declare for 't if you don't favor your gran'ma Dodge's looks. I should like to have yer folks see ye. There, take it off now; I'm most through my ironin' and I want to clear it out o' the way."

Joel was perfectly docile and laid the night-cap within reach. He had a temptation to twitch it back by the end of one string, but he refrained. "Want me to go drive your old brown hen-turkey out o' the wet grass, Mis' Powder? She's tolling her chicks off down to'a'ds the swamp," he offered.

"She's raised up families enough to know how by this time," said Mrs. Powder, "an' the swamp's dry as a bone,"

"I'll split ye up a mess o' kindling-wood whilst I'm here, jest as soon's not," said Joel, in a still more pleasant tone, after a long and anxious pause.

"There, I'll get ye your doughnuts, pretty quick. They ain't so fresh as they was Saturday. I s'pose that's what you're driving at." The good soul shook with laughter. Joe answered as well for her amuse-ment as the most famous of comic actors; there was something in this appealing eyes, his thin cheeks and monstrous freckles, and his long locks of sandy hair, which was very funny to Mrs. Powder. She was always interested, too, in fruitless attempts to satisfy his appetite. He listened now, for the twentieth time, to her opinion that the bottomless pit alone could be compared to the recesses of this being. "I should like to be able to say that I had filled ye up just once!" she ended her remarks, as she brought a tin pan full of doughnuts from her pantry.

"Heard the news?" asked small Joel, as he viewed the provisions with glistening eyes. He bore likeness to a little hungry woodchuck, or muskrat, as he went to work before the tin pan.

"What news?" Mrs. Powder asked, suspiciously. "I ain't seen nobody this day."

"Barnet's folks has got their case in court."

"They ain't!" and while a solemn silence fell upon the kitchen, the belated old clock whirred and rumbled and struck ten with persistent effort. Mrs. Powder looked round at it impatiently; the moon-face confronted her with the same placid smile.

"Twelve o'clock's the time you git your dinner, ain't it, Mis' Powder?" the boy inquired, as if he had repeated his news like a parrot and had no further interest in its meaning.

"I don't plot for to get me no reg'lar dinner this day," was the unexpected reply. "You can eat a couple or three o' them nuts and step along, for all I care. An' I want you to go up Lyddy Bangs's lane and carry her word that I'm goin' out to pick me some blueberries. They 'll be ripened up elegant, and I've got a longin' for 'em. Tell her I say 't is our day—she 'll know; we've be'n after 'arly blueberries together this forty years, and Lyddy knows where to meet with me; there by them split rocks."

The ironing was finished a few minutes afterward, and the board was taken to its place in the shed. When Mrs. Powder returned Joel had stealthily departed; the tin pan was turned upside down on the seat of the kitchen chair. "Good land!" said the astonished woman, "I believe he'll bu'st himself to everlastin' bliss one o' these days. Them doughnuts would have lasted me till Thursday, certain."

"Gimme suthin' to eat, Mis' Powder?" whined Joel at the window, with his plaintive countenance lifted just above the sill. But he set forth immediately down the road, with bulging pockets and the speed of a light-horseman.

II

Half an hour later the little gray farmhouse was shut and locked, and its mistress was crossing the next pasture with a surprisingly quick step for a person of her age and weight. An old cat was trotting after her, with tail high in the air, but it was plain to see that she still looked for danger, having just come down from the woodpile, where she had retreated on Joel's first approach. She kept as close to Mrs. Powder as was consistent with short excursions after crickets or young, unwary sparrows, and opened her wide green eyes fearfully on the lookout for that evil monster, the boy.

There were two pastures to cross, and Mrs. Powder was very much heated by the noonday sun and entirely out of breath when she approached the familiar rendezvous and caught sight of her friend's cape-bonnet.

"Ain't there no justice left?" was her indignant salutation. "I s'pose you 've heard that Crosby's folks have lost their case? Poor Mis' Crosby! 't will kill her, I'm sure. I've be'n calculatin' to go berryin' all the forenoon, but I could n't git word to you till Joel came tootin' by. I thought likely you'd expect notice when you see what a good day 't was."

"I did," replied Lyddy Bangs, in a tone much more serious than her companion's. She was a thin, despairing littler body, with an anxious face and a general look of disappointment and poverty, though really the more prosperous person of the two. "Joel told me you said 't was our day," she added. "I'm wore out tryin' to satisfy that boy; he's always beggin' for somethin' to eat every time he comes nigh the house. I should think they'd see to him to home; not let him batten on the neighbors so."

"You ain't been feedin' of him, too?" laughed Mrs. Powder. "Well, I declare, I don't see whar he puts it!" and she fanned herself with her apron. "I always forget what a sightly spot this is."

"Here 's your pussy-cat, ain't she?" asked Lyddy Bangs, needlessly, as they sat looking off over the valley. Behind them the hills rose one above another, with their bare upland clearings and great stretches of pine and beech forest. Beyond the wide valley was another range of hills, green and pleasant in the clear mid-day light. Some higher mountains loomed, sterile and stony, to northward. They were on the women's right as they sat looking westward.

"It does seem as if folks might keep the peace when the Lord's give 'em so pooty a spot to live in," said Lyddy Bangs, regretfully. "There ain't no better farms than Barnet's and Crosby's folks have got neither, but 'stead o' neighboring they must pick their mean fusses and fight, from generation to generation. My gran'ma'am used to say 't was just so with 'em when she was a girl—and she was one of the first settlers up this way. She al'ays would have it that Barnet's flolks was the most to blame, but there's plenty sides with 'em, as you know."

"There, 't is all mixed up, so 't is—a real tangle," answered Mrs. Powder. "I've been o' both minds— I must say I used to hold for the Crosbys in the old folks' time, but I've come round to see they ain't perfect. There! I'm b'ilin' over with somethin' I've got to tell somebody. I've kep' it close long's I can."

"Let's get right to pickin', then," said Lyddy Bangs, "or we sha'n't budge from here the whole livin' afternoon," and the small thin figure and the tall stout one moved off together toward their well-known harvest-fields. They were presently settled down within good hearing distance, and yet the discussion was not begun. The cat curled herself for a nap on the smooth top of a rock.

"There, I have to eat a while first, like a young-one," said Mrs. Powder. "I always tell 'em that blue-berries is only fit to eat right off of the twigs. You want 'em full o' sun; let 'em git cold and they 're only fit to cook—not but what I eat 'em any ways I can git 'em. Ain't they nice an' spicy? Law, my poor knees is so stiff! I begin to be afraid, nowadays, every year o' berryin' may be my last. I don't know why 't should be that my knees serves me so. I ain't rheumaticky, nor none o' my folks was; we go off with other complaints."

"The mukis membrane o' the knees gits dried up," explained Lyddy Bangs, "an' the j'ints is all powder-posted. So I 've be'n told, anyways."

"Then they was ignorant," retorted her companion, sharply. "I know by the feelin's I have"—and the two friends picked industriously and discussed the vexed points of medicine no more.

"I can't force them Barnets and Crosbys out o' my mind," suggested Miss Bangs after a while, being eager to receive the proffered confidence which might be forgotten. "Think of 'em, without no other door-neighbors, fightin' for three ginerations over the bounds of a lane wall. What if 't was two foot one way or two foot t'other, let 'em agree."

"But that's just what they could n't," said Mrs. Powder. "You know yourself you might be willin' to give away a piece o' land, but when somebody said 't wa'n't yours, 't was theirs, 't would take more Christian grace'n I've got to let 'em see I thought they was right. All the old Crosbys ever wanted, first, was for the Barnets to say two foot of the lane was theirs by rights, and then they was willin' to turn it into the lane and to give that two foot more o' the wedth than Barnets did—they wa'n't haggling for no pay; 't was for rights. But Barnet's folks said"—

"Now don't you go an' git all flustered up a-tellin' that over, Harri't Powder," said the lesser woman. "There ain't be'n no words spoke so often as them along this sidelin' hill, not even the Ten Commandments. The only sense there's be'n about it is, they 've let each other alone altogether, and ain't spoke at all for six months to a time. I can't help hoping that the war'll die out with the old breed and they'll come to some sort of peace. Mis' Barnet was a Sands, and they 're toppin' sort o' folks and she's got fight in her. I think she's more to blame than Barnet, a good sight; but Mis' Crosby's a downright peace-making little creatur', and would have ended it long ago if she'd be'n able."

"Barnet's stubborn, too, let me tell you!" and Mrs. Powder's voice was full of anger. "'T will never die

out in his day, and he'll spend every cent lawing, as
the old folks did afore him. The lawyers must laugh
at him well, 'mongst themselves. One an' another o'
the best on 'em has counseled them to leave it out
to referees, and tried to show 'em they was fools.
My man talked with judge himself about it, once,
after he'd been settin' on a jury and they was comin'
away from court. They could n't agree; they never
could! All the spare money o' both farms has gone
to pay the lawyers and carry on one fight after
another. Now folks don't know it, but Crosby's
farm is all mortgaged; they've spent even what
Mis' Crosby had from her folks. An' there's worse
behind—there's worse behind," insisted the speaker,
stoutly. "I went up there this spring, as you know,
when Mis' Crosby was at death's door with lung-
fever. I went through everything fetchin' of her
round, and was there five weeks, till she got about. 'I
feel to'a'ds you as an own sister,' says Abby Crosby
to me. 'I'm a neighboring woman at heart,' says
she; 'and just you think of it, that my man had to
leave me alone, sick as I was, while he went for you
and the doctor, not riskin' to ask Barnet's folks to
send for help. I like to live pleasant,' says she to me,
and bu'st right out a-cryin'. I knew then how she'd
felt things all these years.—How are they ever goin'
to pay more court bills and all them piles o' damages,
if the farm's mortgaged so heavy?" she resumed.
"Crosby's farm ain't worth a good two thirds of

Barnet's. They've both neglected their lands. How many you got so fur, Lyddy?"

Lyddy proudly displayed her gains of blueberries; the pail was filling very fast, and the friends were at their usual game of rivalry. Mrs. Powder had been the faster picker in years past, and she now doubled her diligence.

"Ain't the sweet-fern thick an' scented as ever you see?" she said. "Gimme pasture-lands rather 'n the best gardins that grows. If I can have a sweet-brier bush and sweet-fern patch and some clumps o' bayberry, you can take all the gardin blooms. Look how folks toils with witch-grass and pusley and gets a starved lot o' poor sprigs, slug-eat, and all dyin' together in their front yards, when they might get better comfort in the first pasture along the road. I guess there's somethin' wild, that's never got tutored out o' me. I must ha' be'n made o' somethin' counter to town dust. I never could see why folks wanted to go off an' live out o' sight o' the mountings, an' have everything on a level."

"You said there was worse to tell behind," suggested Lyddy Bangs, as if it were only common politeness to show an appreciation of the friendly offering.

"I have it in mind to get round to that in proper course," responded Mrs. Powder, a trifle offended by the mild pertinacity. "I settled it in my mind that I was goin' to tell you somethin' for a kind of a treat the day we come out blueberryin'. *There!*"—and Mrs. Powder rose with difficulty from her knees, and retreated pompously to the shade of a hemlock-tree which grew over a shelving rock near by.

Lyddy Bangs could not resist picking a little longer in an unusually fruitful spot; then she hastened to seat herself by her friend. It was no common occasion.

Mrs. Powder was very warm; and further evaded and postponed telling the secret by wishing that she were as light on foot as her companion, and deploring her increasing weight. Then she demanded a second sight of the blueberries, which were compared and decided upon as to quality and quantity. Then the cat, which had been left at some distance on her rock, came trotting toward her mistress in a disturbed way, and after a minute of security in a comfortable lap darted away again in a strange, excited manner.

"She's goin' to have a fit, I do believe!" exclaimed Lyddy Bangs, quite disheartened, for the cat was Mrs. Powder's darling and she might leave everything to go in search of her.

"She may have seen a snake or somethings. She often gets scared and runs home when we 're out a-trarvelin'," said the cat's owner, complacently, and Lyddy's spirits rose again.

"I suppose you never suspected that Ezra Barnet and Ruth Crosby cared the least thing about one another?" inquired the keeper of the secret a moment later, and the listener turned toward Mrs. Powder with a startled face.

"Now, Harri't Powder, for mercy's sakes alive!" was all that she could say; but Mrs. Powder was satisfied, and confirmed, the amazing news by a most emphatic nod.

"My lawful sakes! what be they goin' to do about it?' inquired Lyddy Bangs, flushing with excitement. "A Barnet an' a Crosby fall in love! Don't you rec'lect how the old ones was al'ays fightin' and callin' names when we was all to school together? Times is changed, certain."

"Now, say you hope to die if ever you'll tell a word I say," pursued Mrs. Powder. "If I was to be taken away to-morrow, you 'd be all the one that would know it except Mis' Crosby and Ezra and Ruth themselves. 'T was nothin' but her bein' nigh to death that urged her to tell me that state o' things. I s'pose she thought I might favor 'em in time to come. Abby Crosby she says to me, 'Mis' Powder, my poor girl may need your motherin' care.' An 'I says, 'Mis' Crosby, she shall have it;' and then she had a spasm o' pain, and we harped no more that day as I remember."

"How come it about? I should n't have told anybody that asked me that a Barnet and a Crosby ever 'changed the time o' day, much less kep' company," protested the listener.

"Kep' company! Pore young creatur's!" said Mrs. Powder "They've hid 'em away in the swamps an' hollers, and in the edge o' the growth, at nightfall, for the sake o' gittin a word; an' they've stole out, shiverin', into that plaguy lane o' winter nights. I tell ye I've heard hifalutin' folks say that love would still be lord of all, but I never was 'strained to believe it till I see what that boy and girl was willin' to undergo. All the hate of all their folks is turned to love in them, and I couldn't help a-watchin' of 'em. An' I ventured to send Ruth over to my house after my alpaccy aprin, and then I made an arrant out to the spring-brook to see if there was any cresses started—which I knew well enough there was n't— and I spoke right out bold to Ezra, that was at work on a piece of ditching over on his land. 'Ezra,' says I, 'if you git time, just run over to the edge o' my pasture and pick me a handful o' balm o' Gilead buds. I want to put 'em in half a pint o' new rum for Mis' Crosby, and there ain't a soul to send.' I knew he'd just meet her coming back, if I could time it right gittin' of Ruth started. He looked at me kind of curi's, and pretty quick I see him leggin' it over the fields with an axe and a couple o' ends o' board, like he'd got to mend a fence. I had to keep her dinner warm for her till ha'-past one o'clock. I don't know what he mentioned to his folks, but Ruth she come an' kissed me hearty when she first come inside the door. 'T is harder for Ezra; he ain't got nobody to speak to, and Ruth's got her mother if she is a Mis' Much-afraid."

"I don't know's we can blame Crosby for not wantin' to give his girl to the Barnets, after they've got away all his substance, his means, an' his cattle, like 't was in the Book o' Job," urged Lyddy Bangs. "Seems as if they might call it square an' marry the young folks off, but they won't nohow; 't will only fan the flame." Lyddy Bangs was a sentimental person; neighbor Powder had chosen wisely in gaining a new friend to the cause of Ezra Barnet's apparently hopeless affection. Unknown to herself, however, she had been putting the lover's secret to great risk of untimely betrayal.

The weather was most beautiful that afternoon; there was an almost intoxicating freshness and delight among the sweet odors of the hillside pasture, and the two elderly women were serene at heart and felt like girls again as they talked together. They remembered many an afternoon like this; they grew more and more confiding as they reviewed the past and their life-long friendship. A stranger might have gathered only the most rural and prosaic statements, and a tedious succession of questions, from what Mrs. Powder and Lyddy Bangs had to say to each other, but the old stories of true love and faithful companionship were again simply rehearsed. Those who are only excited by more complicated histories too often forget that there are no new plots to the comedies and tragedies of life. They are played sometimes by country people in homespun, sometimes by townsfolk in velvet and lace. Love and prosperity, death and loss and misfortune—the stories weave themselves over and over again, never mind whether the ploughman or the wit of the clubs plays the part of hero.

The two homely figures sat still so long that they seemed to become permanent points in the landscape, and the small birds, and even a wary chipmunk, went their ways unmindful of Mrs. Powder and Lyddy Bangs. The old hemlock-tree, under which they sat discoursing, towered high above the young pine-growth which clustered thick behind them on the hillside. In the middle of a comfortable reflection upon the Barnet grandfather's foolishness or craftiness, Mrs. Powder gave sudden utterance to the belief that some creature up in the tree was dropping pieces of bark and cones all over her.

"A squirrel, most like," said Lyddy Bangs, looking up into the dense branches. "The tree is a-scatterin' down, ain't it? As you was sayin', Grandsir Barnet must have knowed well enough what he was about"—.

"Oh, gorry! oh, git out! ow—o—w!" suddenly wailed a voice overhead, and a desperate scramble and rustling startled the good women half out of their wits. "Ow, Mis' Powder!" shrieked a familiar voice, while both hearts thumped fast, and Joel came, half falling, half climbing, down out of the tree. He bawled, and beat his head with his hands, and at last rolled in agony among the bayberry and lamb-kill. "Look out for 'em!" he shouted. "Oh, gorry! I thought 't was only an old last-year's hornet's nest—they 'll sting you, too!"

Mrs. Powder untied her apron and laid about her with sure aim. Only two hornets were to be seen; but after these were beaten to the earth, and she stopped to regain her breath, Joel hardly dared to lift his head or to look about him.

"What was you up there for, anyhow?" asked Lyddy Bangs, with severe suspicion. "Harking to us, I'll be bound!" But Mrs. Powder, who knew Joel's disposition best, elbowed her friend into silence and began to inquire about the condition of his wounds. There was a deep-seated hatred between Joel and Miss Bangs.

"Oh, dear! they've bit me all over," groaned the boy. "Ain't you got somethin' you can rub on, Mis' Powder?"—and the rural remedy of fresh earth was suggested.

"'T is too dry here," said the adviser. "Just you step down to that ma'shy spot there by the brook, dear, and daub you with the wet mud real good, and 't will ease you right away." Mrs. Powder's voice sounded compassionate, but her spirit and temper of mind gave promise of future retribution.

"I 'll teach him to follow us out eavesdropping, this fashion! " said Lyddy Bangs, when the boy had departed, weeping. "I'm more 'n gratified that the hornets got hold of him! I hope 't will serve him for a lesson."

"Don't you r'ile him up one mite, now," pleaded Mrs. Powder, while her eyes bore witness of hardly controlled anger. "He's the worst tattle-tale I ever see, and we've put ourselves into a trap. If he tells his mother she 'll spread it all over town. But I should no more thought o' his bein' up in that tree than o' his bein' the sarpent in the garden o' Eden. You leave Joel to me, and be mild with him 's you can."

The culprit approached, still lamenting. His ear and cheek were hugely swollen already, so that one eye was nearly closed. The blueberry expedition was relinquished, and with heavy sighs of dissatisfaction Lyddy Bangs took up the two half-filled pails, while Mrs. Powder kindly seized Joel by his small, thin hand, and the little group moved homeward across the pasture.

"Where's your hat?" asked Lyddy, stopping short, after they had walked a little distance.

"Hanging on a limb up by the wop's nest," answered Joel. "Oh, git me home, Mis' Powder!"

III

No one would suspect, from the look of the lane itself, that it had always been such a provoker of wrath, and even a famous battle-ground. While petty wars had raged between the men and women of the old farms, walnut-trees had grown high in air, and apple-trees had leaned their heavy branches on the stone walls and, year after year, decked themselves in pink-and-white blossoms to arch this unlucky by-way for a triumphal procession of peace that never came. Birds built their nests in the boughs and pecked the ripe blackberries; green brakes and wild roses and tall barberry-bushes flourished in their season on either side the wheel-ruts. It was a remarkably pleasant country lane, where children might play and lovers might linger. No one would imagine that this lane had its law-suits and damages, its annual crop of briefs, and succession of surveyors and quarrelsome partisans; or that in every generation of owners each man must be either plaintiff or defendant.

The surroundings looked permanent enough. No one would suspect that a certain piece of wall had been more than once thrown down by night and built again, angrily, by day; or that a well-timbered corn-house had been the cause of much litigation, and even now looked, when you came to know its story, as if it stood on its long, straight legs, like an ungainly, top-heavy beast, all ready to stalk away when its position became too dangerous. The Barnets had built it beyond their boundary; it had been moved two or three times, backward and forward.

The Barnet house and land stood between the Crosby farm and the high-road; the Crosbys had never been able to reach the highway without passing their enemies under full fire of ugly looks or taunting voices. The intricacies of legal complications in the matter of right of way would be impossible to explain. They had never been very clear to any impartial investigator. Barnets and Crosbys had gone to their graves with bitter hatred and sullen desire for revenge in their hearts. Perhaps this one great interest, outside the simple matters of food and clothing and farmers' work, had taken the place to them of drama and literature and art. One could not help thinking, as he looked at the decrepit fences and mossy, warped roofs and buckling walls, to how much better use so much money might have been put. The costs of court and the lawyers' fees had taken everything, and men had drudged, in heat and frost, and women had pinched and slaved to pay the lane's bills. Both the Barnet and Crosby of the present time stood well enough in the opinion of other neighbors. They were hard-fisted, honest men; the fight was inherited to begin with, and they were stubborn enough to hold fast to the fight. Law Lane was as well known as the county roads in half a dozen towns. Perhaps its irreconcilable owners felt a thrill of enmity that had come straight down from Scottish border-frays, as they glanced along its crooked length. Who could believe that the son and daughter of the warring households, instead of being ready to lift the torch in their turn, had weakly and misguidedly fallen in love with each other?

Nobody liked Mrs. Barnet. She was a cross-grained, suspicious soul, who was a tyrant and terror of discomfort in her own household whenever the course of events ran counter to her preference. Her son Ezra was a complete contrast to her in disposition, and to his narrow-minded, prejudiced father as well. The elder Ezra was capable of better things, however, and might have been, reared to friendliness and justice, if the Crosby of his youthful day had not been specially aggravating and the annals of Law Lane at their darkest page. If there had been another boy to match young Ezra, on the Crosby farm, the two might easily have fostered their natural boyish rivalries until something worse came into being; but when one's enemy is only a sweet-faced little girl, it is very hard to impute to her all manner of discredit and serpent-like power of evil. At least, so Ezra Barnet the younger felt in his inmost heart; and though he minded his mother for the sake of peace, and played his solitary games and built his unapplauded dams and woodchuck-traps on his own side of the fences, he always saw Ruth Crosby as she came and went, and liked her better and better as years went by. When the tide of love rose higher than the young people's steady heads, they soon laid fast hold of freedom. With all their perplexities, life was by no means at its worst, and rural diplomacy must bend all its energies to hinder these unexpected lovers.

Ezra Barnet had never so much as entered the Crosby house; the families were severed beyond the reuniting power of even a funeral. Ezra could only try to imagine the room to which his Ruth had returned one summer evening after he had left her, reluctantly, because the time drew near for his father's return from the village. His mother had been in a peculiarly bad temper all day, and he had been glad to escape from her unwelcome insistence that he should marry any one of two or three capable girls, and so furnish some help in the housekeeping. Ezra had often heard this suggestion of his duty, and, tired and provoked at last, he had stolen out to the garden and wandered beyond it to the brook and out to the fields. Somewhere, somehow, he had met Ruth, and the lovers bewailed their trials with unusual sorrow and impatience. It seemed very hard to wait. Young Barnet was ready to persuade the tearful girl that they must go away together and establish a peaceful home of their own. He was heartily ashamed because the last verdict was in his father's favor, and Ruth forebore to wound him with any glimpse of the straits to which her own father had been reduced. She was too dutiful to leave the pinched household, where her help was needed more than ever; she persuaded her lover that they were sure to be happy at last—indeed, were not they happy now? How much worse it would be if they could not safely seize so many opportunities, brief though they were, of being together! If the fight had been less absorbing and the animosity less bitter, they might have been suspected long ago.

So Ruth and Ezra parted, with uncounted kisses, and Ezra went back to the dingy-walled kitchen, where his mother sat alone. It was hardly past twilight out of doors, but Mrs. Barnet had lighted a kerosene-lamp, and sat near the small open window mending a hot-looking old coat. She looked so needlessly uncomfortable and surly that her son was filled with pity, as he stood watching her, there among the moths and beetles that buffeted the lamp-chimney.

"Why don't you put down your sewing and come out a little ways up the road, mother, and get cooled off?" he asked, pleasantly; but she only twitched herself in her chair and snapped off another needleful of linen thread.

"I can't spare no time to go gullivantin', like some folks," she answered. "I always have had to work, and I always shall. I see that Crosby girl mincin' by an hour ago, as if she 'd be'n off all the afternoon. Folks that think she 's so amiable about saving her mother's strength would be surprised at the way she dawdles round, I guess"—and Mrs. Barnet crushed an offending beetle with her brass thimble in a fashion that disgusted Ezra. Somehow, his mother had a vague instinct that he did not like to hear sharp words about Ruth Crosby. Yet he rarely had been betrayed into an ill-judged defense. He had left Ruth only a minute ago; he knew exactly what she had been doing all day, and from what kind errand she had been returning; the blood rushed quickly to his face, and he rose from his seat by the table and went out to the kitchen doorstep. The air was cool and sweet, and a sleepy bird chirped once or twice from an elm-bough overhead. The moon was near its rising, and he could see the great shapes of the mountains that lay to the eastward. He forgot his mother, and began to think about Ruth again; he wondered if she were not thinking of him, and meant to ask her if she remembered an especial feeling of nearness just at this hour. Ezra turned to look at the clocks to mark the exact time.

"Yes," said Mrs. Barnet, as she saw him try to discover the hour, " 't is time that father was to home. I s'pose, bein' mail-night, everybody was out to the post-office to hear the news, and most like he's bawlin' himself hoarse about fall 'lections or something. He ain't got done braggin' about our gittin' the case, neither. There's always some new one that wants to git the p'ints right from headquarters. I didn't see Crosby go by, did you? "

"He'd have had to foot it by the path 'cross-lots," replied Ezra, gravely, from the doorstep. " He's sold his hoss."

"He ain't! "exclaimed Mrs. Barnet, with a chuckle. "I s'pose they 're proddin' him for the money up to court. Guess he won't try to fight us again for one while."

Ezra said nothing; he could not bear this sort of thing much longer. "I won't be kept like a toad under a harrow," he muttered to himself. "I think it seems kind of hard," he ventured to say aloud. "Now he 's got to hire when fall work comes on, and"—

The hard-hearted woman within had long been trying to provoke her peaceable son into an argument, and now the occasion had come. Ezra restrained himself from speech with a desperate effort, and stopped his ears to the sound of his mother's accusing voice. In the middle of her harangue a wagon was driven into the yard, and his father left it quickly and came toward the door.

"Come in here, you lout!" he shouted, angrily. "I want to look at you! I want to see what such a mean-spirited sneak has got to say for himself." Then changing his voice to a whine, he begged Ezra, who had caught him from falling as he stumbled over the step, " Come in, boy, an' tell me 't ain't true. I guess they was only thornin' of me up; you ain't took a shine to that Crosby miss, now, have you?"

"No son of mine—no son of mine!" burst out the mother, who had been startled by the sudden entrance of the news-bringer. Her volubility was promptly set free, and Ezra looked from his father's face to his mother's.

"Father," said he, turning away from the scold, who was nearly inarticulate in her excess of rage—"father, I'd rather talk to you, if you want to hear what I've got to say. Mother's got no reason in her."

"Ezry," said the elder man, " I see how 't is. Let your ma'am talk all she will. I'm broke with shame of ye!"—his voice choked weakly in his throat. "Either you tell me 't is all nonsense, or you go out o' that door and shut it after you for good. An' ye 're all the boy I've got."

The woman had stopped at last, mastered by the terror of the moment. Her husband's face was gray with passion; her son's cheeks were flushed and his eyes were full of tears. Mrs. Barnet's tongue for once had lost its cunning.

The two men looked at each other as long as they could; the younger man's eyes fell first. "I wish you would n't be hasty," he said; "to-morrow"—

"You've heard," was the only answer; and in a moment more Ezra Barnet reached to the table and took his old straw hat which lay there.

"Good-by, father!" he said, steadily. "I think you 're wrong, sir; but I never meant to carry on that old fight and live like the heathen." And then, young and strong and angry, he left the kitchen.

"He might have took some notice o' me, if he 's goin' for good," said the mother spitefully; but her son did not hear this taunt, and the father only tottered where he stood. The moths struck against his face as if it were a piece of wood; he sank feebly into a chair, muttering, and trying to fortify himself in his spent anger.

Ezra went out, dazed and giddy. But he found the young horse wandering about the yard, eager for his supper and fretful at the strange delay. He unharnessed the creature and backed the wagon under the shed; then he turned and looked at the house— should he go in? No! The fighting instinct, which had kept firm grasp on father and grandfather, took possession of Ezra now. He crossed the yard and went out at the gate, and down the lane's end to the main road. The father and mother listened to his footsteps, and the man gave a heavy groan.

"Let him go —let him go! 't will teach him a lesson!" said Mrs. Barnet, with something of her usual spirit She could not say more, though she tried her best; the occasion was far too great.

How many times that summer Mrs. Powder attempted to wreak vengeance upon Joel, the tattle-tale; into what depths of intermittent remorse the mischief-making boy was resolutely plunged, who shall describe? No more luncheons of generous provision; no more jovial skirmishing at the kitchen windows, or liberal payment for easy errands. Whenever Mrs. Powder saw Lyddy Bangs, or any other intimate and sympathetic friend, she bewailed her careless confidences under the hemlock-tree and detailed her anxious attentions to the hornet-stung eavesdropper.

"I went right home," she would say, sorrowfully; "I filled him plumb-full with as good a supper as I could gather up, and I took all the fire out o' them hornit-stings with the best o' remedies. 'Joel, dear,' says I, 'you won't lose by it if you keep your mouth shut about them words I spoke to Lyddy Bangs,' and he was that pious I might ha' known he meant mischief. They ain't boys nor men, they're divils, when they come to that size, and so you mark my words! But his mother never could keep nothing to herself, and I knew it from past sorrers; and I never slept a wink that night—sure's you live—till the roosters crowed for day."

"Perhaps 't won't do nothin' but good!" Lyddy Bangs would say, consolingly. "Perhaps the young folks 'll git each other a sight the sooner. They 'd had to kept it to theirselves till they was gray-headed, less somebody let the cat out o' the bag."

"Don't you rec'lect how my cat acted that day!"

exclaimed Mrs. Powder, excitedly. "How she was good as took with a fit! She knowed well enough what was brewin'; I only wish we 'd had half of her sense."

I V

The day before Christmas all the long valley was white with deep, new-fallen snow. The road which led up from the neighboring village and the railroad station stretched along the western slope—a mere trail, untrodden and unbroken. The storm had just ceased; the high mountain-peaks were clear and keen and rose-tinted with the waning light; the hills were no longer green with their covering of pines and maples and beeches, but gray with bare branches, and a cold, dense color, almost black, where the evergreens grew thickest. On the other side of the valley the farmsteads were mapped out as if in etching or pen-drawing; the far-away orchards were drawn with a curious exactness and regularity, the crooked boughs of the apple-trees and the longer lines of the walnuts and ashes and elms came out against the snow with clear beauty. The fences and walls were buried in snow; the farm-houses and barns were petty shapes in their right-angled unlikeness to natural growths. You were half amused, half shocked, as the thought came to you of indifferent creatures called men and women, who busied themselves within those narrow walls, under so vast a sky, and fancied the whole importance of the universe was belittled by that of their few pent acres. What a limitless world lay outside those play-thing-farms, yet what beginnings of immortal things the small gray houses had known!

The day before Christmas!—a festival which seemed in that neighborhood to be of modern origin. The observance of it was hardly popular yet among the elder people, but Christmas had been appropriated, nevertheless, as if everybody had felt the lack of it. New Year's Day never was sufficient for New England, even in its least mirthful decades. For those persons who took true joy in life, something deeper was needed than the spread-eagle self-congratulations of the Fourth of July, or the family reunions of Thanksgiving Day. There were no bells ringing which the country-folks in Law Lane might listen for on Christmas Eve; but something more than the joy that is felt in the poorest dwelling when a little child, with all its possibilities, is born; something happier still came through that snowy valley with the thought of a Christmas-Child who "was the bringer-in and founder of the reign of the higher life." This was the greater Thanksgiving Day, when the whole of Christendom is called to praise and pray and hear the good-tidings, and every heart catches something of the joyful inspirations of good-will to men.

Ezra Barnet sat on a fallen tree from which he had brushed the powdery snow. It was hard work wading through the drifts, and he had made good headway up the long hill before he stopped to rest. Across the valley in the fading daylight he saw the two farms, and could even trace the course of Law Lane itself, marked by the well-known trees. How small his own great nut-tree looked at this distance. The two houses, with their larger and smaller outbuildings and snow-topped woodpiles, looked as if they had crept near together for protection and companionship. There were no other houses within a wide space. Ezra knew how remote the homes really were from each other, judged by any existing sympathy and interest. He thought of his bare, unnourished boyhood with something like resentment; then he remembered how small had been his parents' experience, what poor ambition had been fostered in them by their lives; even his mother's impatience with the efforts he had made to bring a little more comfort and pleasantness to the old farm-house was thought of with pity for her innate lack of pleasure in pleasant things. Ezra himself was made up of inadequacies, being born and bred of the Barnets. He was at work on the railroad now, with small pay; but he had always known that there could be something better than the life in their farmhouse, while his mother did not. A different feeling came over him as he thought whom the other farm-house sheltered; he had looked for that first, to see if it were standing safe. Ruth's last letter had come only the day before. This Christmas holiday was to be a surprise to her. He wondered whether Ruth's father would let him in.

Never mind! he could sleep in the barn among the hay; and Ezra dropped into the snow again from the old tree-trunk and went his way. There was a small house just past a bend in the road, and he quickened his steps toward it. Alas! there was no smoke in Mrs. Powder's chimney. She was away on one of her visiting tours; nursing some sick person, perhaps. She would have housed him for the night most gladly; now he must take his chances in Law Lane.

The darkness was already beginning to fall; there was a curious brownness in the air, like summer twilight; the cold air became sharper, and the young man shivered a little as he walked. He could not follow the left-hand road, where it led among hospitable neighbors, but turned bravely off toward his old home—a long, lonely walk at any time of the year, among woods and thickets all well known to him, and as familiar as they were to the wild creatures that haunted them. Yet Ezra Barnet did not find it easy to whistle as he went along.

Suddenly, from behind a scrub-oak that was heavily laden with dead leaves and snow, leaped a small figure, and Ezra was for the moment much startled. The boy carried a rabbit-trap with unusual care, and placed it on the snow-drift before which he stood waist-deep already. "Gorry, Ezry! You most scared me to pieces!" said Joel, in a perfectly calm tone. "Wish you Merry Christmas! Folks 'll be lookin' for you; they did n't s'pose you 'd git home before to-morrow, though."

"Looking for me?" repeated the young man, with surprise. "I did n't send no word"—

"Ain't you heard nothin' 'bout your ma'am's being took up for dead?"

"No, I ain't; and you ain't foolin' me with your stories, Joel Smith? You need n't play off any of your mischief into me."

"What you gittin' mad with me about?" inquired Joel, with a plaintive tone in his voice. "She got a fall out in the barn this mornin', an' it liked to killed her. Most folks ain't heard nothin' 'bout it 'cause its been snowin' so. They come for Mis' Powder and she called out to our folks, as they brought her round by the way of Asa Packer's store to git some opodildack or somethin'."

Ezra asked no more questions, but strode past the boy, who looked after him a moment, and then lifted the heavy box-trap and started homeward. The imprisoned rabbit had been snowed up since the day before at least, and Joel felt humane anxieties, else he would have followed Ezra at a proper distance and learned something of his reception.

Mrs. Powder was reigning triumphant in the Barnet house, being nurse, housekeeper, and spiritual adviser all in one. She had been longing for an excuse to spend at least half a day under that cheerless roof for many months, but occasion had not offered. She found the responsibility of the parted lovers weighing more and more heavily on her mind, and had set her strong will at work to find some way of reuniting them, and even to restore a long-banished peace to the farms. She would not like to confess that a mild satisfaction caused her heart to feel warm and buoyant when an urgent summons had come at last; but such was the simple truth. A man who had been felling trees on the farm brought the news, melancholy to hear under other circumstances, that Mrs. Barnet had been hunting eggs in a stray nest in the hay-mow, and had slipped to the floor and been taken up insensible. Bones were undoubtedly broken; she was a heavy woman, and had hardly recovered her senses. The doctor must be found as soon as possible. Mrs. Powder hastily put her house to rights, and, with a good round bundle of what she called her needments, set forth on the welcome enterprise. On the way she could hardly keep herself from undue cheerfulness,

and if ever there was likely to be a reassuring presence in a sick-room it was Harriet Powder's that
December day.

She entered the gloomy kitchen looking like a
two-footed snow-drift, her big round shoulders were
so heaped with the damp white flakes. Old Ezra
Barnet sat by the stove in utter despair, and waved a
limp hand warningly toward the bedroom door.

"She 's layin' in a sog," he said, hopelessly, "I
ought-to thought to send word to pore Ezry—all
the boy she ever had,"

Mrs. Powder calmly removed her snowy outer
garments, and tried to warm her hands over the fire.

"Put in a couple o' sticks of good dry wood," she
suggested, in a soothing voice; and the farmer felt
his spirits brighten, he knew not why. Then the
whole-souled, hearty woman walked into the bedroom.

"All I could see," she related afterward, "was the
end of Jane Barnet's nose, and I was just as sure then
as I be now that she was likely to continner; but I
set down side of the bed and got holt of her hand,
and she groaned two or three times real desperate.
I wished the doctor was there, to see if anything
really ailed her; but I someways knowed there
wa'n't, 'less 't was gittin' over such a jounce. I spoke
to her, but she never said nothin', and I went back
out into the kitchen. 'She's a very sick woman,' says
I, loud enough for her to hear me; I knew 't would

please her. There was good deal to do, and I put on my aprin and took right holt and begun to lay about me and git dinner; the men-folks was wiltin' for want o' somethin', it being nigh three o'clock. An' then I got Jane to feel more comfortable with ondressin' of her, for all she'd hardly let me touch of her—poor creatur', I expect she did feel sore!—and then daylight was failin' and I felt kind o' spent, so I set me down in a cheer by the bed-head and was speechless, too. I knew if she was able to speak she could n't hold in no great spell longer.

"After a while she stirred a little and groaned, and then says she, 'Ain't the doctor comin'?' And I peaced her up well 's I could. 'Be I very bad off, Harri't?' says she.

" 'We'll hope for the best, Jane,' says I; and that minute the notion come to me how I'd work her round, an' I like to laughed right out, but, I did n't.

" 'If I should lose me again, you must see to sendin' for my son,' says she; 'his father's got no head.'

" 'I will,' says I, real solemn. 'An' you can trust me with anything you feel to say, sister Barnet.'

"She kind of opened her eye that was next to me and surveyed my countenance sharp, but I looked serious, and she groaned real honest. 'Be I like old Mis' Topliff?' she whispered, and I kind o' nodded an' put my hand up to my eyes. She *was* like her, too; some like her, but not nigh so bad, for Mis'

Topliff was hurt so fallin' down the sullar-stairs that she never got over it an' died the day after.

"'Oh, my sakes!' she bu'st out whinin', 'I can't be took away now. I ain't a-goin' to die right off, be I, Mis' Powder?'

"'I ain't the one to give ye hope. In the midst of life we are in death. We ain't sure of the next minute, none of us,' says I, meanin' it general, but discoursin' away like an old book o' sermons.

"'I do feel kind o' failin', now,' says she. 'Oh, can't you do nothin'?'—and I come over an' set on the foot o' the bed an' looked right at her. I knew she was a dreadful notional woman, and always made a fuss when anything was the matter with her; could n't bear no kind o' pain.

"'Sister Barnet,' says I, 'don't you bear nothin' on your mind you'd like to see righted before you go? I know you ain't been at peace with Crosby's folks, and 't ain't none o' my business, but I should n't want to be called away with hard feelin's in *my* heart. You must overlook my speaking right out, but I should want to be so used myself.'

"Poor old creatur'! She had an awful fight of it, but she beat her temper for once an' give in. 'I do forgive all them Crosbys,' says she, an' rolled up her eyes. I says to myself that wa'n't all I wanted, but I let her alone a spell, and set there watchin' as if I expected her to breathe her last any minute.

"She asked for Barnet, and I said he was anxious and out watchin' for the doctor, now the snow'd stopped. 'I wish I could see Ezra,' says she. 'I'm all done with the lane now, and I'd keep the peace if I was goin' to live.' Her voice got weak, and I did n't know but she was worse off than I s'posed. I was scared for a minute, and then I took a grain o' hope. I'd watched by too many dyin'-beds not to know the difference.

" 'Don't ye let Barnet git old Nevins to make my coffin, will ye, Mis' Powder?' says she once.

" 'He's called a good workman, ain't he?' says I, soothin' as I could. When it come to her givin' funeral orders, 't was more 'n I could do to hold in.

" 'I ain't goin' snappin' through torment in a hemlock coffin, to please that old cheat!' says she, same's if she was well, an' ris' right up in bed; and then her bruises pained her an' she dropped back on the pillow.

" 'Oh, I'm a-goin' now!' says she. 'I've been an awful hard woman. 'T was I put Barnet up to the worst on 't. I'm willin' Ezra should marry Ruthy Crosby; she's a nice, pooty gal, and I never owned it till now I'm on my dyin'-bed—Oh, I'm a-goin', I'm a-goin'!—Ezra can marry her, and the two farms together 'll make the best farm in town. Barnet ain't got no fight left; he's like an old sheep since we drove off Ezra.' And then she'd screech; you never saw no such a fit of narves. And the end was I had to send to Crosby's, in all the snow, for them to come over.

"An' Barnet was got in to hold her hand and hear last words enough to make a Fourth o' July speech; and I was sent out to the door to hurry up the Crosbys, and who should come right out o' the dark but Ezra. I declare, when I see him you could a-knocked me down with a feather. But I got him by the sleeve—'You hide away a spell,' says I, 'till I set the little lamp in this winder; an' don't you make the best o' your ma's condition; 'pear just as consarned about her as you can. I 'll let ye know why, soon's we can talk'—and I shoved him right out an' shut the door.

"The groans was goin' on, and in come Crosby and Ruth, lookin' scared about to death themselves. Neither on 'em had ever been in that house before, as I know of. She called 'em into the bedroom and said she'd had hard feelin's towards them and wanted to make peace before she died, and both on 'em shook hands with her.

" 'Don't you want to tell Ruth what you said to me about her and Ezry?' says I, whisperin' over the bed. "Live or dead, you know 't is right and best.'

" 'There ain't no half way 'bout me,' she says, and so there wa'n't. 'Ruth,' says she, out loud, 'I want you to tell pore Ezra that I gave ye both my blessin',' and I made two steps acrost that kitchen and set the lamp in the window, and in comes

Ezra—pore boy, he did n't know what was brewin', and thought his mother was dyin' certain when he saw the Crosbys goin' in.

"He went an' stood beside the bed, an' his father clutched right holt of him. Thinks I to myself, if you make as edifyin' an end when your time really does come, you may well be thankful, Jane Barnet!

"They was all a-weepin', an' I was weepin' myself, if you 'll believe it, I'd got a-goin' so. You ought to seen her take holt o' Ruth's hand an' Ezra's an' put 'em together. *Then* I'd got all I wanted, I tell you. An' after she'd screeched two or three times more she begun to git tired; the poor old creatur' was shook up dreadful, and I felt for her consid'able, though you may not think it; so I beckoned 'em out into the kitchen an' went in an' set with her alone. She dropped off into a good easy sleep, an' I told the folks her symptoms was more encouragin'.

"I tell you, if ever I took handsome care o' any sick person 't was Jane Barnet, before she got about again; an' Ruth she used to come over an' help real willin'. She got holt of her ma'-in-law's bunnit one afternoon an' trimmed it up real tasty, and that pleased Mis' Barnet about to death. My conscience pricked me some, but not a great sight. I'm willin' to take what blame come to me by rights.

"The doctor come postin' along, late that night, and said she was doin' well, owin' to the care she'd had, and give me a wink. And she's alive yet," Mrs.

Powder always assured her friends, triumphantly—
"and, what's more, is middlin' peaceable disposed.
She's said one or two p'inted things to me, though,
an' I should n't wonder, come to think it over, if she
mistrusted me just the least grain. But, dear sakes!
they never was so comfortable in their lives; an'
Ezra he got a first-rate bargain for a lot o' Crosby's
woodland that the railroad wanted, and peace is kind
o' set in amon'st 'em up in Law Lane."

V

When Ezra Barnet waked on Christmas morning,
in his familiar, dark little chamber under the lean-to
roof, he could hardly believe that he was at home
again, and that such strange things had happened.
There were cheerful voices in the kitchen below,
and he dressed hurriedly and went downstairs.

There was Mrs. Powder, cooking the breakfast
with lavish generosity, and beaming with good-
nature. Barnet, the father, was smiling and looking
on with pleased antcipation; the sick woman was
comfortably bolstered up in the bedroom. In all his
life the son had never felt so drawn to his mother;
there was a new look in her eyes as he went toward
her; she had lost her high color, and looked at him
pleadingly, as she never had done before, "Ezry,
come close here!" said she. "I believe I'm goin' to
git about ag'in, after all. Mis' Powder says I be; but

them feelin's I had slippin' down the mow, yesterday, was twice as bad as the thump I struck with. I may never be the same to work, but I ain't goin' to fight with folks no more, sence that Lord 'll let me live a spell longer. I ain't a-goin' to fight with nobody, no matter how bad I want to. Now, you go an' git you a good breakfast. I ain't eat a mouthful since break-fast yesterday, and you can bring me a help o' any-thing Sister Powder favors my havin'."

"I hope 't will last," muttered Sister Powder to herself, as she heaped the blue plate. "Wish you all a Merry Christmas!" she said. "I like to forgot my manners."

It was Christmas Day, whether anybody in Law Lane remembered it or not. The sun shone bright on the sparkling snow, the eaves were dropping, and the snow-birds and blue-jays came about the door. The wars of Law Lane were ended.

Turkeys and a Footrace

[HENRY A. SHUTE]

D id you ever think that one of the main reasons of the difficulty our farmers have of realizing more than a moderate competency from the cultivation of a New England farm is the want of a good market?

The cities and large towns are few in number and so small, and the Boston markets for farm products of the perishable kinds are supplied by the larger, nearer, and more fertile farms and market gardens of suburban towns.

But for hardy perennials, such as chickens, ducks, lambs, goats, calves, and woodchucks, there is, and ever has been, a fairly good market, and much money has been made in the cultivation of such products.

Thirty or forty years ago, and as far prior thereto as the memory of man runneth, even to the time the first white man landed in America and on the solar plexus of the amber-hued aborigine, the sound of the turkey was heard in the land and vied with the song of the birds, the nasal tones of the lusty husbandman berating his sluggish cattle, the bleating of sheep, the lowing of cattle, and the grunting and squealing of fat pigs, all of which went to make up a pastoral symphony or bucolic *tout ensemble*. Daily the flock of bronze beauties descended to the fields and woods, where they industriously put in from twelve to fourteen working hours in hunting down grasshoppers, katydids, crickets, and other vermin, and nightly did they festoon the apple trees, the roofs of sheds and barns, and the seats of farm-wagons with their plump bodies.

In those days the raising and marketing of turkeys formed one of the principal sources of income for the farmer or the farmer's helpmeet. They were raised in two ways. The most profitable method was to enter your neighbor's orchard when the family were asleep, and carefully and without noise raise the drowsy turkeys from their roosting places, and market them in a distant county before morning broke.

The element of chance that entered into the transaction and occasionally involved those interested in this industry in expensive legal proceedings rendered this method slightly unpopular, although the percentage of profit was very considerable.

The other and more popular method was to allow the woman of the household to take entire charge of the flock, and to hold the proceeds for her personal use and adornment.

To this circumstance the beautiful sables that have been handed down in country families owe their origin. Our grandmothers, great- and great-great-grandmothers developed great fleetness of foot in avoiding the lightning charge of irate cock-turkeys weighing forty or more pounds, and a wide range of geographical knowledge in seeking and housing the immature flocks when a rain-cloud appeared on the horizon.

Indeed, many of our long-distance pedestrians and short-distance sprinters of to-day have come to their full powers by a careful cultivation of a direct inheritance from athletic great-great-grandmothers. But of late years turkey-raising as a local industry has not flourished, and the New Hampshire turkey is almost extinct.

What is the reason? One has it that the increasing liberality of the modern farmer husband is such that his wife obtains her heart's desire simply for the asking, and is not obliged to raise live-stock for a living. Another, that marriages between the different sexes in the turkey family have been allowed within those degrees of consanguinity that in the human species are prohibited by law, and the result has been the production of a race of turkey degenerates predisposed to paresis, suicide, and kindred ills.

Still another says that an insect known as the borer, equipped with a cast-iron, auger-like proboscis, working on a swivel, bores holes in the bird's crop and lets its contents exude with the innocent life of the victim.

This man affirms that another insect bores into the ears of the young bird and drives it to suicide. One says it is over-feeding, another starvation. One advises leaving the birds to nature, another, highly artificial measures. It reminds me of the old definition of climate as given by our old friend Guyot's "Common School Geography."

"Climate is heat and cold, moisture and dryness, healthfulness or unhealthfulness." I well remember my childish wonder that one term could embrace so many contrary characteristics.

In thinking matters over, I finally became convinced that the opportunity had arrived to make my name, like that of our national emblem, "known and honored throughout the world." To invent, discover, and develop, to patent or copyright a process for preserving the life of the New Hampshire turkey, was to put it into the power of every farmer to remove the mortgage from his ancestral acres, to put money in his purse, to give his daughters lessons in elocution, and to allow his wife to join the "Daughters," and to live happy ever afterwards. Perhaps as "Shute, the turkey man," my name might go pinwheeling through the ages to come, neck and neck with the names of Buffalo Jones, Scroggs the Wyandotte man, the inventor of Mennen's Toilet Powder, and kindred celebrities.

So I invested in a pair of mammoth bronzes that were displayed in a window of a Boston store, and awaited their arrival with ill-concealed anxiety.

For three nights subsequent to the purchase of the birds I drove to the station with a huge crate, which I had fastened to the pung so firmly that it prevented me from using the sleigh for any other purpose, and for three nights I returned disappointed. On the fourth night I found them waiting in a crate fully as large, upon which freight-bills were due sufficient to freight a horse to the Pacific slope. This, with the amount already paid for the birds, made my original investment somewhat disquieting. However, I loaded the new crate on the old one, tied it as well as I could with the hitch-rope, climbed stiffly to the seat, and started for home.

Respected reader, did you ever try to drive a hard-bitted horse with one hand and hold in two crates weighing about a ton each, and laden with shifting ballast in the shape of agile and wildly terrified turkeys? It is a trick, let me tell you. I covered the distance between the station and my house in several seconds less than the record, and pulled both arms a foot or more beyond their normal reach while so doing.

I was so anxious to release my turkeys that I neglected to unhook the mare, and when after considerable difficulty I dragged forth the cock-turkey by
one hind-leg, he beat my hat over my ears with his
huge wings, covered me with dust and dirt, and so
frightened the mare that she went through the narrow door like a flash of lightning, leaving a pung
with broken shafts and a goodly part of the harness
on the outside.

I was too much occupied with the turkey to pay
much attention to the mare, and after a brief season
of collar-and-elbow, Græco-Roman, hitch-and-trip,
and catch-as-catch-can, I dragged the unwilling old
bird from his retirement, left him in the loft, swelling
and spreading, and dashed down after the hen, suddenly reflecting that I had left the crate open.

I found her standing in the open, with outstretched neck and tail half-spread. Awed by my
commanding appearance, or possibly by the fact
that I had so many feathers on me that she mistook
me for a strange turkey-cock of disreputable appearance, she started off at a high rate of speed and I
followed at a hand-gallop. The going was heavy and
I soon overtook her, fell over her prostrate body,
half-buried in the snow, and arose with her clasped
to my bosom.

Before I could catch her by the legs she, with ill-
directed but vigorous clawings, gouged a long strip
from my countenance, leaving an unsightly scar that

remained for several weeks, and gave rise to the rumor that my home life was unhappy.

She was not nearly as handsome or as heavy as her mate, but that she was dear to him he demonstrated by furiously attacking me when I appeared in the loft, and tearing a large hole in my trousers, in return for which I kicked him several yards with some considerable deftness, and left him to smooth his ruffled plumage and temper, while I sought warm water, Pears' soap, court-plaster, and a clothes-brush.

As it was early in March, when cock-turkeys are about as savage as four-year-old Jersey bulls, I warned the different members of our family to give him the right of way.

I soon found that he was at heart a most pusillanimous poltroon, for a small gamecock that roosted in the loft, so far from being terrified by his appearance and loud boasts, thoroughly whipped him, and drove him headlong down one of the grain chutes, whence we rescued him by tearing away the planks, empurpled and nearly dead from a rush of blood to the head.

Although an arrant coward, he put up such a menacing front, boasted so loudly, and turned so red-faced in his anger that he impressed the members of my family, the neighbors, and the populace generally, as a very dangerous antagonist.

My daughter, like her father extraordinarily gifted in the way of legs, had no difficulty in distancing the old fellow, and dodging his fierce rushes, and the daily sight of a very funny young lady with spindly legs flying across the yard pursued by a red-faced, gobbling turkey, added much to the interest with which the neighborhood viewed him.

My wife, however, had no patience with the young lady or any one else who was afraid of an old turkey, and expressed great confidence that the day old Tom came at her would be a very sad day for the poor old fellow. This naturally made me look forward to the inevitable meeting between the mistress of the house and the master of the yard as a prospective treat.

One day I was in the barn and saw the usual stern chase swinging its way across the yard. Scarcely had the house-door slammed before it opened again, and there strode forth, with firm step and resolute manner, the lady of the house with the light of high purpose and the glint of warlike determination beaming through her specs. The old cock had retired some distance from the house, but drew up as the apparition approached.

As the meeting promised to be of some interest, I peeped through a window and prepared to get as much enjoyment out of the engagement as the nature of the circumstances would allow.

Straight toward old Tom came the lady with rapid and measured strides. Instantly he hoisted his tail, injected about a quart of scarlet war-paint into his head and neck, stuck every feather on end, and let out a fierce rolling gobble. The walk slowed down a bit, and the lady cut her smile of confidence down one half, but still advanced warily.

The gobbler then made a whining imitation of a watchman's rattle, laid the feathers of his neck flat until his head looked snaky, and took a few side steps toward his visitor.

"Shoo, you nasty thing! Shoo!! scat!!! go away!!!!" screamed the lady, stopping abruptly.

Old Tom whined like a dog, ending with a sort of bass croak that seemed to come from the pit of his stomach, then took a few more steps forward on tiptoe, and sounded the watchman's rattle, winding up with a fierce gobble.

"Go away, you nasty thing! Shoo!! scat!!!" shrieked the lady. "Oh, why don't somebody come? Oh-ee!! Oh-ee!! Get away!!" she shrieked vigorously, and somewhat improperly shaking her skirts, with marked scenic effect.

This was the chip on the shoulder, the challenge that an adult male turkey always takes up. With outstretched neck and hideous whine he charged, and with shrill shrieks the lady fled for the friendly shelter of the open portal. I have ridden on the "Flying Yankee," I have flashed down the toboggan slide, have shot or "shooted" the chutes, have twice been run away with when astride a bronco, have seen the fastest sprinter breast the tape in an even ten, have seen the two-minute pacer coming down the stretch abreast the thoroughbred runners, but never have I seen such a burst of speed as my wife put on that day. She fairly whizzed across the yard and disappeared into the house like a flash of jagged lightning, and the bang with which she slammed the door, echoed and reëchoed and drowned my coarse and unfeeling laughter and the delighted giggle of my irreverent daughter, who from a convenient window had viewed the proceedings with great enjoyment. Truly this turkey business was not a bad investment after all.

As spring approached, my turkey began to lay large pock-marked eggs with exceedingly rough shells, which I carefully secured and concealed from the prying eyes of the cook.

As soon as I had a sufficient number, I set them under two large fluffy hens and sternly repressed the maternal instinct of the turkey-hen, daily removing her forcibly, protestingly, flappingly from her nest under a pile of brush, where she persistently sat on a couple of bricks. In due time the eggs under the hens hatched and the bricks under the turkey refused to hatch, but the enthusiasm of the old turkey-hen continued unabated. She seemed determined to hatch out terra cotta images, drain-tile, or something.

The little turks or poults were delightful little wild things, beautifully mottled, and on them I lavished the affection of a warm and ardent nature. On one of them, as an experiment, I lavished something even more ardent, for under the advice of a Granger friend I introduced a pepper-corn into the epiglottis of an infant turk and watched the effect. It was instantaneous. The poor bird piped a shrill protest, turned flip-flaps, hand-springs, and cart-wheels, opened its beak, clawed at it with frenzied feet, rolled, ran, fell, and finally collapsed into a piteous little ball of down and died.

This experiment, at least, was not a success, except as an exterminator, and I had but fifteen poults instead of the original sixteen. I then put them in a well-sheltered place and fed them according to the best standards.

For a while all went well. They grew and throve, and I became very complacent over the matter. Too much so, I am afraid, for on my return from the office one day I found three of them suffering from melancholia, with heads sunk on their breasts, and apparently indifferent to their surroundings. I at once powdered them thoroughly with insect powder, under which drastic treatment they promptly died without struggle or squeak.

A week later, four more passed peacefully away without apparent reason, and a week later cholera attacked the remainder. One by one they passed to the great hereafter. We found them in all places, in all positions. Some on their backs, with their feeble little claws outstretched in air, some huddled into corners, with heads drawn back over their shoulders, some curled up like balls of fur.

In vain I tried all the remedies in the poultry papers and in books. In vain I consulted wise sages and oracles in poultry-culture. It was useless; those turks were doomed from the moment of their entrance into a sinful world. In a month from their arrival nothing remained but bitter memories and a very inconsiderable addition to my compost-heap.

In the meantime the old cock, having much unoccupied time on his hands, and pining for the society of his wife, who was still sitting on the bricks under the brush-heap, was occupied in chasing defenseless women from the premises. Scarcely a day passed without a sally and a rescue.

In his blundering, well-meaning way he was doing a deal of good. The female book agent and subscription fairy fled from my premises as from a place accursed. The dark-complexioned lady of Armenian extraction, with big feet and still bigger suitcase, crowded to the brim with gaudy and useless wares, was driven from the premises instanter. The saturnine villain with parti-colored rugs had to fly for his life. The small boys, who had worn a path through my lawn to the campus, were forced to pass through a neighbor's garden, and the D'Indy Club, the Frauenverein, the Mothers' Club, the committee on church affairs, met elsewhere.

Really, I was quite ready to repeat my experiment should anything happen to my old friend, and stood ready to advocate the cock-turkey as the watch-dog of the household.

One day, as I was passing the brush-heap, I be-thought myself of taking a look at the turkey-hen. So I pulled her hissing from her nest, and to my sur-prise found that the bricks had been pushed from the nest, and in their place were eight eggs. With a thrill at my heart that reminded me of my boyish days of birds'-egging, I replaced her carefully and took heart again.

Perhaps I had made a mistake after all. Perhaps the books were wrong. I remembered to have heard a story once of an Irish common councilman, who in a somewhat acrimonious debate as to how many gondolas should be bought for the pond in a pub-lic park, sturdily advocated the purchase of a male gondola and a female gondola, "an' t' lave th' rist t' nature," as a measure calculated to minimize expense.

Would it not be better to discontinue the artificial methods and "lave th' rist t' nature"? I would try. It could n't be any worse. I could n't lose any more than the whole brood. Could n't I? Wait a bit.

In due time every egg hatched, and the mother turkey cautiously crept out, suspicious of every sound, watchful of every movement. That night they disappeared in a grove back of my lot.

The next morning I arose betimes, or a full hour and a half before betimes, and stole into the silent wood. Joy! at the foot of a huge pine I found her and her tiny babies, safe, sound, and dry, although a smart shower had left everything dripping.

It was a success. She alone had the secret of nature. Away with artificial methods. Return to nature. Strange how besotted man gets in his ignorance. But for blind adherence to experiment, the New Hampshire turkey

"Might have stood against the world,

  Now none so poor to do him reverence."

Wait a bit: that night at dusk I stole again into the forest, and to the foot of that mighty pine. She was not there, neither were her chicks.

The mother love, suspicious, primeval, alert, had prompted her to find a new hiding-place. I would pit my wits against hers. Not to interfere with nature, but to keep her in sight, to study her cunning, to learn her secret.

I hunted so long that night that on my return in the darkness I bumped into trees and stubs,—

"I scratched my hands, and tore my hair,

  But still did not complain."

The next morning at daybreak, and the next night at dusk, and for many, many weary days and nights, I searched, and peered, and sneaked, and spied, and climbed trees, and skinned and barked and abraded myself in various tender places.

"Donati lived, and long you might have seen
An old man wandering as in search of something,
Something he could not find, he knew not what."

In vain my search. I never saw her again, nor did I ever see her chicks, and to this day their disappearance is a mystery.

It seemed to me that the old cock sympathized with my grief. At least he did not seem the same turkey, and he began to follow me around. It may have been that he was considering the advisability of giving me a poke with his iron beak. But if so, he never did.

Time passed. The haying season arrived, waxed, and waned. Green corn, astrachan apples, Sanford's Jamaica Ginger, and allopathic physicians battled for the lives of our dear ones; Colorado beetles cut my potato-tops to the ground, rose-bugs in flying swarms devastated my "jacks." In short, from morning to night the whole household was engaged in a hand-to-hand struggle to rescue our feeble crops from their many enemies. Constant occupation is good for grief and disappointment.

In due time my cheerfulness returned. Old Tom conceived a violent passion for a diminutive bantam hen, and the memory of his erring or unfortunate mate faded.

September came with its early crops, but I had no crops. October with its later harvests, but I gathered none. November merged into December; December into January. Old Tom began with the lengthening days to develop a savage temper. An early February storm had made ponds of our garden, and sharp weather had converted it into a fine rink, where my daughter spent her leisure hours.

Shortly after the noon hour I was in my room, disrobed. I had just finished caring for my stable animals. Suddenly a series of loud screams startled me. I rushed to the window, pulled up the shade, and looked. Penned into a corner cowered my small daughter, while before her, scarlet of neck, swollen of wattles, with every feather on end, towered old Tom, furious and menacing.

From the side porch the housemaid screamed hysterical advice, and jumped up and down in her excitement.

I grabbed my trousers. They were wrong-side-out, and I got stuck in them, and fell to the floor. Gentle reader, did you ever try to pull on your trousers while the house was burning, and when the salvation of yourself or your loved ones depended upon speed? Try it some time and see how adroit you are. I threw them across the room, got on one shoe, and was groping under the bed for the other, when another cry of terror electrified me, and I dashed for the stairs.

"For heaven's sake, are n't you going to put on some clothes?" screamed my wife; "the girl is out there."

"Damn the girl!" I snapped; "if she can stand there and see that gobbler scare Nath. to death, I guess it won't hurt her to see me." And I shot down the stairs like an Andover quarterback going through a hole in the Exeter line.

"The uniform 'e wore
  Was nothin' much afore
  An' rather less than 'alf o' that be'ind."

I grasped a broom as I flew through the kitchen, turned the corner of the shed on one wheel, and dashed into the open with a whoop. At the unexpected appearance of so skinny a spectre clad in pale mauve underwear, stretched to its utmost tension by frantic straddles, the housemaid shrieked and threw her apron over her head, but I kept on. Arrived in time, I swung with all my strength on the gobbler's scarlet neck, but missed, and turning several times with the momentum, fell and rolled on the ice.

I fairly bounced to my feet and dashed after the flying bird. Down the field we went, round the apple trees, the gobbler in the lead, just out of reach. Through the rose-bushes, which tore ravelings from my underwear and cuticle from my straining legs; round by the shed the chase continued, over the wood-pile, which turned and rolled on me, giving the gobbler a fresh start.

But I picked myself up. I did not feel my bruises. Eliza crossing the ice was not more oblivious of her cut and naked feet. I was going to catch that gobbler if I broke something. No red-headed devil bird should menace the life of the child of my old age; and again I picked up my agile heels and flew. This time the wily old bird took me over a hard-frozen corn-field with stubs, but failed to shake me off.

Neighbors threw up the windows and stared. People in passing teams stopped and cheered us on. The bird ran with drooping wings. He was about all in. So was I. Suddenly he stopped and squatted. I tried to stop, but could not, and fell with soul-shaking violence.

When I sat up, the gobbler had crawled into the barn, and with the assistance of my wife and daughter, who draped me in a table-cloth, I returned to my room, regained my breath gradually, and resumed my clothing.

Does any one wish to but an adult male turkey? Weighs thirty pounds; is a direct descendant of the first turkey seen by the Pilgrim. Fathers when they moored their bark on the wild New England shore.

It may be the original turkey. I can't say. Turkeys are not in general valuable on account of their antiquity, but a genuine Stradivarius turkey, with Sheraton legs, Hepplewhite upholstery, and Chippendale varnish, of undoubted antiquity and undisputed ancestry, ought to bring a good price. At any rate, the turkey industry on the D. F. Ranch is hereby discontinued.

The Calf—Another Footrace

[HENRY A. SHUTE]

Experienced farmers have all united in an opinion that a cow should go dry at least six weeks before the calf comes. This serves a double purpose. The cow gets a rest and a chance to recuperate from the strain of giving a pint of milk in a ten-quart pail twice a day, and the merry farmer has six weeks to get the cramps out of his hands, caused by trying to get the cow to part with that pint of milk, and the stain out of his soul, caused by his lying about the amount.

In this way much good is done to the old line-back and to the old moss-back, and both are bene-fited to a very great degree. The cow grows fat on good food and inaction, but the farmer grows thin-ner, if possible, because one source of income, to-wit the milk, is cut off.

However, as I was assured that this was the proper thing, I was determined to carry it out at all hazards. I didn't just know how to go to work. If the cow had been addicted to smoking, I could have made her smoke rattan, which, as every boy knows, dries up the blood, and, of course, could have no other effect upon the milk.

This being out of the question, I then thought of giving her doses of alum. You see, when I was a boy and had a canker in my mouth, which was always explained to me by my mother as being the direct result of saying bad words, and which for many good reasons I could not deny, a little alum rubbed on the affected part puckered up my lips so that they looked like the stem end of a green tomato, and made my mouth so dry that I couldn't spit through my teeth, another accomplishment of mine, for a week. But how I could whistle!

Naturally, this occurred to me as a facile means of drying up the old cow, but before putting it in operation I consulted the fountainhead of all bucolic knowledge, Daniel, my rosy and jocose neighbor.

"How much milk does she give?" queried Daniel, in answer to my request for instructions.

"About a pint and a half," I replied.

"Dry! How much drier do you expect to get her?" exclaimed Daniel with some heat. "If I had a cow that didn't give but a pint at a milking, I should think she was pretty almighty dry. You don't want to endanger your premises by getting her so dry that you can't take a lantern into the barn, do you?"

"Well, no," I replied doubtfully, "but I want her dry."

"Don't milk her to-morrow," said Daniel.

So the next morning I omitted to milk her, and before noon my wife was in tears, three small children in the neighborhood had convulsions and five complaints were entered to the proper authorities that I was maintaining a nuisance in keeping a bellowing cow.

So at noon I milked her and got a quart. Then I went to Daniel again.

"Don't feed her," said Daniel.

So that noon I didn't fill the manger, but tied her under an open shed. Before night, several old ladies in the neighborhood were taken with nervous prostration, and I was served with a *quo warranto,* a *mandamus,* a *ne exeat regno,* a notice of a hearing on a petition for an injunction, a libel for divorce, and arrested on a warrant on a complaint charging me with conspiracy to make a tumult in the compact part of the village.

As the last-mentioned instrument was returnable before my own court, I did not worry about it, but hastily fed the querulous and bellowing animal, and returned to my office where I drew up as an answer to the other actions: "Necessarium est quod non potest aliter se habere." This calmed my mind somewhat. I had at least got some cases on the docket to defend.

I then returned to Daniel.

"Damn the cow!" said Daniel.

"That don't amount to anything," I replied, "I have done that for months."

"Kill her then," he retorted, and washed his hands of the affair.

This was perhaps the best advice he had given, but I couldn't bring myself to do violence to so old and tried a chum. We had had too many wildly exciting times together. She was rough, but I always could depend on her to do the best she could and give me a square tussle.

In due time the calf came and was pronounced a beauty. He—much to my regret it was a he—did not seem exactly handsome or shapely. On the contrary, he seemed a sprawling heap of awkward, bony, wobbly legs.

Indeed, he spent the best part of the first day in awkward attempts to rise, and prodigious successes in the way of heavy crumpled-up tumbles. But in a few days, Moses! how that calf could run, kick and butt.

We naturally had a little reception for it. You see, a calf is a new thing to us and we were proud of it,—her,—him, I mean. So one day as I was exhibiting it,—him—to several neighbors, he reached forward, caught hold of a button on my vest, just over the pit of my stomach, and mouthed it in the most cunning manner. I held my breath so as not to scare it, and the ladies were in ecstasies. I did not hold my breath long, however, for suddenly the animal, with the natural intent to increase the flow of milk, gave me a terrific bunt with its nose, in which all the weight of its body and all the convulsive power of its suddenly stiffened legs were expended.

All the breath in my body was expelled with such violence that I only regained it after a paroxysm of hoarse gasps and startling hawks, which antics and involuntary inch-wormings, I am sorry to say, entertained my callers far more than the antics of the calf.

When the calf was three weeks old, it had developed speed of a race-horse quality and frequently dragged me about the premises with unparalleled swiftness, and at the end of a stout rope. This was good exercise for both of us, and kept down the increasing flesh of over-maturity.

One day, as I was coming from the office, I saw the calf coming down the street from my premises at a wild gallop, flinging up his heels and dragging a long rope. I was not quick enough to head him off, but with rare presence of mind jumped with both feet on the rope as the animal shot by me like a flash of lightning. When I lit I was nearly a rod from the starting-place and on my head and shoulders. People who saw me in the air said I looked like a pinwheel, so rapid were my revolutions.

I was mad! Thoroughly mad! Fighting mad! I would catch that devilish calf if I burst something; and I took up the running.

Scientists say that the wild ass of the desert is the swiftest of all animals. Be it so; but without desiring to institute any comparisons, I must acknowledge that a certain tame one developed the most astonishing burst of speed on Pine and Front Streets on that day that ever drew the attention of the sporting world.

Round the corner of Pine and Front we went, I on one wheel and the calf heeling dangerously to leeward and with its keel half out of water.

Righting ourselves, we flew along like International Cup winners. In front of the Seminary entrance, by terrific sprinting, I had nearly closed the gap between us. From the Seminary entrance to Tan Lane the calf drew away from me, as my spark-plug fell out or my carbureter failed to carburet.

At the lower part of the Academy yard I was almost within reach of my opponent's rudder, but failed to grasp it. Suddenly he tacked abruptly into Elm Street, while I skidded to Conner's fence and ripped off a tire, but kept on with frantic grasping jumps. Just in front of the Unitarian Church I had made up my lost space, when the calf suddenly stopped and we came together like two football tackles, amid a cloud of dust. I had run down my prize.

As I slowly returned up Front Street, breathless but triumphant, I received many laughing congratulations over my fleetness and determination. Just as I was about to reënter my yard, I heard Daniel from his piazza across the way shout, "Say, old man, no end obliged to you for bringing back my calf. Saved me lots of trouble. Let the man hitch him in my barn, please."

Sure enough, a glance showed my calf lying quietly under a tree, safely tethered to a crowbar, while I had chased his infernal calf over two miles at race-horse speed. In a sort of daze I handed the grinning man the rope, looked at my torn and dusty clothes, my shoe with the sole gone and my ruined hat.

"Curse your calf!" I hissed, and limped painfully into my house.

An Old-Fashioned Thanksgiving

[**LOUISA MAY ALCOTT**]

November, 1881

Sixty years ago, up among the New Hampshire hills, lived Farmer Bassett, with a houseful of sturdy sons and daughters growing up about him. They were poor in money, but rich in land and love, for the wide acres of wood, corn, and pasture land fed, warmed, and clothed the flock, while mutual patience, affection, and courage made the old farm-house a very happy home.

November had come; the crops were in, and barn, buttery, and bin were overflowing with the harvest that rewarded the summer's hard work. The big kitchen was a jolly place just now, for in the great fire-place roared a cheerful fire; on the walls hung garlands of dried apples, onions, and corn; up aloft from the beams shone crook-necked squashes, juicy hams, and dried venison—for in those days deer still haunted the deep forests, and hunters flourished. Savory smells were in the air; on the crane hung steaming kettles, and down among the red embers copper saucepans simmered, all suggestive of some approaching feast.

A white-headed baby lay in the old blue cradle that had rocked six other babies, now and then lifting his head to look out, like a round, full moon, then subsided to kick and crow contentedly, and suck the rosy apple he had no teeth to bite. Two small boys sat on the wooden settle shelling corn for popping, and picking out the biggest nuts from the goodly store their own hands had gathered in October. Four young girls stood at the long dresser, busily chopping meat, pounding spice, and slicing apples; and the tongues of Tilly, Prue, Roxy, and Rhody went as fast as their hands. Farmer Bassett, and Eph, the oldest boy, were "chorin' 'round" outside, for Thanksgiving was at hand, and all must be in order for that time-honored day.

To and fro, from table to health, bustled buxom Mrs. Bassett, flushed and floury, but busy and blithe as the queen bee of this busy little hive should be.

"I do like to begin seasonable and have things to my mind. Thanksgivin' dinners can't be drove, and it does take a sight of victuals to fill all these hungry stomicks," said the good woman, as she gave a vigorous stir to the great kettle of cider apple-sauce, and cast a glance of housewifely pride at the fine array of pies set forth on the buttery shelves.

"Only one more day and then it will be the time to eat. I didn't take but one bowl of hasty pudding this morning, so I shall have plenty of room when the nice things come," confided Seth to Sol, as he cracked a large hazel-nut as easily as a squirrel.

"No need of my starvin' beforehand. *I always* have room enough, and I'd like to have Thanksgiving every day," answered Solomon, gloating like a young ogre over the little pig that lay near by, ready for roasting.

"Sakes alive, I don't, boys! It's a marcy it don't come but once a year. I should be worn to a thread-paper with all this extra work atop of my winter weavin' and spinnin'," laughed their mother, as she plunged her plump arms into the long bread-trough and began to knead the dough as if a famine were at hand.

Tilly, the oldest girl, a red-cheeked, black-eyed lass of fourteen, was grinding briskly at the mortar, for spices were costly, and not a grain must be wasted. Prue kept time with the chopper, and the twins sliced away at the apples till their little brown arms ached, for all knew how to work, and did so now with a will.

"I think it's real fun to have Thanksgiving at home. I'm sorry Gran'ma is sick, so we can't go there as usual, but I like to mess 'round here, don't you, girls?" asked Tilly, pausing to take a sniff at the spicy pestle.

"It will be kind of lonesome with only our own folks." "I like to see all the cousins and aunts, and have games, and sing," cried the twins, who were regular little romps, and could run, swim, coast, and shout as well as their brothers.

"I don't care a mite for all that. It will be so nice to eat dinner together, warm and comfortable at home," said quiet Prue, who loved her own cozy nooks like a cat.

"Come, girls, fly 'round and get your chores done, so we can clear away for dinner jest as soon as I clap my bread into the oven," called Mrs. Bassett presently, as she rounded off the last loaf of brown bread which was to feed the hungry mouths that seldom tasted any other.

"Here's a man comin' up the hill lively!" "Guess it's Gad Hopkins. Pa told him to bring a dezzen oranges, if they warn't too high!" shouted Sol and Seth, running to the door, while the girls smacked their lips at the thought of this rare treat, and Baby threw his apple overboard, as if getting ready for a new cargo.

But all were doomed to disappointment, for it was not Gad, with the much-desired fruit. It was a stranger, who threw himself off his horse and hurried up to Mr. Bassett in the yard, with some brief message that made the farmer drop his ax and look so sober that his wife guessed at once some bad news had come; and crying, "Mother's wuss! I know she is!" out ran the good woman, forgetful of the flour on her arms and the oven waiting for its most important batch.

The man said old Mr. Chadwick, down to Keene, stopped him as he passed, and told him to tell Mrs. Bassett her mother was failin' fast, and she'd better come to-day. He knew no more, and having delivered his errand he rode away, saying it looked like snow and he must be jogging, or he wouldn't get home till night.

"We must go right off, Eldad. Hitch up, and I'll be ready in less'n no time," said Mrs. Bassett, wasting not a minute in tears and lamentations, but pulling off her apron as she went in, with her head in a sad jumble of bread, anxiety, turkey, sorrow, haste, and cider apple-sauce.

A few words told the story, and the children left their work to help her get ready, mingling their grief for "Gran'ma" with regrets for the lost dinner.

"I'm dreadful sorry, dears, but it can't be helped. I couldn't cook nor eat no way now, and if that blessed woman gets better sudden, as she has before, we'll have cause for thanksgivin', and I'll give you a dinner you won't forget in a hurry," said Mrs. Bassett, as she tied on her brown silk pumpkin-hood, with a sob for the good old mother who had made it for her.

Not a child complained after that, but ran about helpfully, bringing moccasins, heating the foot-stone, and getting ready for a long drive, because Gran'ma lived twenty miles away, and there were no railroads in those parts to whisk people to and fro like magic. By the time the old yellow sleigh was at the door, the bread was in the oven, and Mrs. Bassett was waiting, with her camlet cloak on, and the baby done up like a small bale of blankets.

"Now, Eph, you must look after the cattle like a man, and keep up the fires, for there's a storm brewin', and neither the children nor dumb critters must suffer," said Mr. Bassett, as he turned up the collar of his rough coat and put on his blue mittens, while the old mare shook her bells as if she pre-ferred a trip to Keene to hauling wood all day.

"Tilly, put extry comfortables on the beds to-night, the wind is so searchin' up chamber. Have the baked beans and Injun-puddin' for dinner, and whatever you do, don't let the boys git at the mince-pies, or you'll have them down sick. I shall come back the minute I can leave Mother. Pa will come to-morrer anyway, so keep snug and be good. I depend on you, my darter; use your jedgment, and don't let nothin' happen while Mother's away."

"Yes'm, yes'm—good-bye, good-bye!" called the children, as Mrs. Bassett was packed into the sleigh and driven away, leaving a stream of directions behind her.

Eph, the sixteen-year-old boy, immediately put on his biggest boots, assumed a sober, responsible manner, and surveyed his little responsibilities with a paternal air, drolly like his father's. Tilly tied on her mother's bunch of keys, rolled up the sleeves of her homespun gown, and began to order about the younger girls. They soon forgot poor Granny, and found it great fun to keep house all alone, for Mother seldom left home, but ruled her family in the good old-fashioned way. There were no servants, for the little daughters were Mrs. Bassett's only maids, and the stout boys helped their father, all working happily together with no wages but love; learning in the best manner the use of the heads and hands with which they were to make their own way in the world.

The few flakes that caused the farmer to predict bad weather soon increased to a regular snowstorm, with gusts of wind, for up among the hills winter came early and lingered long. But the children were busy, gay, and warm in-doors, and never minded the rising gale nor the whirling white storm outside.

Tilly got them a good dinner, and when it was over the two elder girls went to their spinning, for in the kitchen stood the big and little wheels, and baskets of wool-rolls, ready to be twisted into yarn for the winter's knitting, and each day brought its stint of work to the daughters, who hoped to be as thrifty as their mother.

Eph kept up a glorious fire, and superintended the small boys, who popped corn and whittled boats on the hearth; while Roxy and Rhody dressed corn-cob dolls in the settle corner, and Bose, the brindled mastiff, lay on the braided mat, luxuriously warming his old legs. Thus employed, they made a pretty picture, these rosy boys and girls, in their homespun suits, with the rustic toys or tasks which most children nowadays would find very poor or tiresome.

Tilly and Prue sang, as they stepped to and fro, drawing out the smoothly twisted threads to the musical hum of the great spinning-wheels. The little girls chattered like magpies over their dolls and the new bed-spread they were planning to make, all white dimity stars on a blue calico ground, as a Christmas present to Ma. The boys roared at Eph's jokes, and had rough and tumble games over Bose, who didn't mind them in the least; and so the afternoon wore pleasantly away.

At sunset the boys went out to feed the cattle, bring in heaps of wood, and lock up for the night, as the lonely farm-house seldom had visitors after dark. The girls got the simple supper of brown bread and milk, baked apples, and a doughnut all 'round as a treat. Then they sat before the fire, the sisters knitting, the brothers with books or games, for Eph loved reading, and Sol and Seth never failed to play a few games of Morris with barley corns, on the little board they had made themselves at one corner of the dresser.

"Read out a piece," said Tilly from Mother's chair, where she sat in state, finishing off the sixth woolen sock she had knit that month.

"It's the old history book, but here's a bit you may like, since it's about our folks," answered Eph, turning the yellow page to look at a picture of two quaintly dressed children in some ancient castle.

"Yes, read that. I always like to hear about the Lady Matildy I was named for, and Lord Bassett, Pa's great-great-great-grandpa. He's only a farmer now, but it's nice to know we were somebody two or three hundred years ago," said Tilly, bridling and tossing her curly head as she fancied the Lady Matilda might have done.

"Don't read the queer words, 'cause we don't understand 'em. Tell it," commanded Roxy, from the cradle, where she was drowsily cuddled with Rhody.

"Well, a long time ago, when Charles the First was in prison, Lord Bassett was a true friend to him," began Eph, plunging into his story without delay. "The lord had some papers that would have hung a lot of people if the king's enemies got hold of 'em, so when he heard one day, all of a sudden, that soldiers were at the castle-gate to carry him off, he had just time to call his girl to him, and say: 'I may be going to my death, but I won't betray my master. There is no time to burn the papers, and I can not take them with me; they are hidden in the old leathern chair where I sit. No one knows this but you, and you must guard them till I come or send you a safe messenger to take them away. Promise me to be brave and silent, and I can go without fear.' You see, he wasn't afraid to die, but he *was* to seem a traitor. Lady Matildy promised solemnly, and the words were hardly out of her mouth when the men came in, and her father was carried away a prisoner and sent off to the Tower."

"But she didn't cry; she just called her brother, and sat down in that chair, with her head leaning back on those papers, like a queen, and waited while the soldiers hunted the house over for 'em: wasn't that a smart girl?" cried Tilly, beaming with pride, for she was named for this ancestress, and knew the story by heart.

"I reckon she was scared, though, when the men came swearin' in and asked her if she knew anything about it. The boy did his part then, for *he* didn't know, and fired up and stood before his sister; and he says, says he, as bold as a lion: 'If my lord had told us where the papers be, we would die before we would betray him. But we are children and know nothing, and it is cowardly of you to try to fight us with oaths and drawn swords!' "

As Eph quoted from the book, Seth planted himself before Tilly, with the long poker in his hand, saying, as he flourished it valiantly:

"Why didn't the boy take his father's sword and lay about him? I would, if any one was ha'sh to Tilly."

"You bantam! he was only a bit of a boy, and couldn't do anything. Sit down and hear the rest of it," commanded Tilly, with a pat on the yellow head, and a private resolve that Seth should have the largest piece of pie at dinner next day, as reward for his chivalry.

"Well, the men went off after turning the castle out of window, but they said they should come again; so faithful Matildy was full of trouble, and hardly dared to leave the room where the chair stood. All day she sat there, and at night her sleep was so full of fear about it, that she often got up and went to see that all was safe. The servants thought the fright had hurt her wits, and let her be, but Rupert, the boy, stood by her and never was afraid of her queer ways. She was 'a pious maid,' the book says, and often spent the long evenings reading the Bible, with her brother by her, all alone in the great room, with no one to help her bear her secret, and no good news of her father. At last, word came that the king was dead and his friends banished out of England. Then the poor children were in a sad plight, for they had no mother, and the servants all ran away, leaving only one faithful old man to help them."

"But the father did come?" cried Roxy, eagerly.

"You'll see," continued Eph, half telling, half reading.

"Matilda was sure he would, so she sat on in the big chair, guarding the papers, and no one could get her away, till one day a man came with her father's ring and told her to give up the secret. She knew the ring, but would not tell until she had asked many questions, so as to be very sure, and while the man answered all about her father and the king, she looked at him sharply. Then she stood up and said, in a tremble, for there was something strange about the man: 'Sir, I doubt you in spite of the ring, and I will not answer till you pull off the false beard you wear, that I may see your face and know if you are my father's friend or foe.' Off came the disguise, and Matilda found it was my lord himself, come to take them with him out of England. He was very proud of that faithful girl, I guess, for the old chair still stands in the castle, and the name keeps in the family, Pa says, even over here, where some of the Bassetts came along with the Pilgrims."

"Our Tilly would have been as brave, I know, and she looks like the old picter down to Gran'ma's, don't she, Eph?" cried Prue, who admired her bold, bright sister very much.

"Well, I think you'd do the settin' part best, Prue, you are so patient. Till would fight like a wild cat, but she can't hold her tongue worth a cent," answered Eph; whereat Tilly pulled his hair, and the story ended with a general frolic.

When the moon-faced clock behind the door struck nine, Tilly tucked up the children under the "extry comfortables," and having kissed them all around, as Mother did, crept into her own nest, never minding the little drifts of snow that sifted in upon her coverlet between the shingles of the roof, nor the storm that raged without.

As if he felt the need of unusual vigilance, old Bose lay down on the mat before the door, and pussy had the warm hearth all to herself. If any late wanderer had looked in at midnight, he would have seen the fire blazing up again, and in the cheerful glow the old cat blinking her yellow eyes, as she sat bolt upright beside the spinning-wheel, like some sort of household goblin, guarding the children while they slept.

When they woke, like early birds, it still snowed, but up the little Bassetts jumped, broke the ice in their jugs, and went down with cheeks glowing like winter apples, after a brisk scrub and scramble into their clothes. Eph was off to the barn, and Tilly soon had a great kettle of mush ready, which, with milk warm from the cows made a wholesome breakfast for the seven hearty children.

"Now about dinner," said the young house-keeper, as the pewter spoons stopped clattering, and the earthen bowls stood empty.

"Ma said, have what we liked, but she didn't expect us to have a real Thanksgiving dinner, because she won't be here to cook it, and we don't know how," began Prue, doubtfully.

"I can roast a turkey and make a pudding as well as anybody, I guess. The pies are all ready, and if we can't boil vegetables and so on, we don't deserve any dinner," cried Tilly, burning to distinguish herself, and bound to enjoy to the utmost her brief authority.

"Yes, yes!" cried all the boys, "let's have a dinner anyway; Ma won't care, and the good victuals will spoil if they ain't eaten right up."

"Pa is coming to-night, so we won't have dinner till late; that will be real genteel and give us plenty of time," added Tilly, suddenly realizing the novelty of the task she had undertaken.

"Did you ever roast a turkey?" asked Roxy, with an air of deep interest.

"Should you darst to try?" said Rhody, in an awe-stricken tone.

"You will see what I can do. Ma said I was to use my judgment about things, and I'm going to. All you children have got to do is to keep out of the way, and let Prue and me work. Eph, I wish you'd put a fire in the best room, so the little ones can play in there. We shall want the settin'-room for the table, and I won't have them pickin' 'round when we get things fixed," commanded Tilly, bound to make her short reign a brilliant one.

"I don't know about that. Ma didn't tell us to,"

began cautious Eph who felt that this invasion of the sacred best parlor was a daring step.

"Don't we always do it Sundays and Thanksgivings? Wouldn't Ma wish the children kept safe and warm anyhow? Can I get up a nice dinner with four rascals under my feet all the time? Come, now, if you want roast turkey and onions, plum-puddin' and mince-pie, you'll have to do as I tell you, and be lively about it."

Tilly spoke with such spirit, and her suggestion was so irresistible, that Eph gave in, and, laughing good-naturedly, tramped away to heat up the best room, devoutly hoping that nothing serious would happen to punish such audacity.

The young folks delightedly trooped away to destroy the order of that prim apartment with housekeeping under the black horse-hair sofa, "horseback-riders" on the arms of the best rocking-chair, and an Indian war-dance all over the well-waxed furniture. Eph, finding the society of peaceful sheep and cows more to his mind than that of two excited sisters, lingered over his chores in the barn as long as possible, and left the girls in peace.

Now Tilly and Prue were in their glory, and as soon as the breakfast-things were out of the way, they prepared for a grand cooking-time. They were handy girls, though they had never heard of a cooking-school, never touched a piano, and knew nothing of embroidery beyond the samplers which hung framed in the parlor; one ornamented with a pink mourner under a blue weeping-willow, the other with this pleasing verse, each word being done in a different color, which gave the effect of a distracted rainbow:

This sampler neat was worked by me,

In my twelfth year, Prudence B.

Both rolled up their sleeves, put on their largest aprons, and got out all the spoons, dishes, pots, and pans they could find, "so as to have everything handy," Prue said.

"Now, sister, we'll have dinner at five; Pa will be here by that time, if he is coming to-night, and be so surprised to find us all ready, for he won't have had any very nice victuals if Gran'ma is so sick," said Tilly, importantly. "I shall give the children a piece at noon" (Tilly meant luncheon); "doughnuts and cheese, with apple-pie and cider, will please 'em. There's beans for Eph; he likes cold pork, so we won't stop to warm it up, for there's lots to do, and I don't mind saying to you I'm dreadful dubersome about the turkey."

"It's all ready but the stuffing, and roasting is as easy as can be. I can baste first-rate. Ma always likes to have me, I'm so patient and stiddy, she says," answered Prue, for the responsibility of this great undertaking did not rest upon her, so she took a cheerful view of things.

"I know, but it's the stuffin' that troubles me," said Tilly, rubbing her round elbows as she eyed the immense fowl laid out on a platter before her. "I don't know how much I want, nor what sort of yarbs to put in, and he's so awful big, I'm kind of afraid of him."

"I ain't! I fed him all summer, and he never gobbled at *me*. I feel real mean to be thinking of gobbling him, poor old chap," laughed Prue, patting her departed pet with an air of mingled affection and appetite.

"Well, I'll get the puddin' off my mind fust, for it ought to bile all day. Put the big kettle on, and see that the spit is clean, while I get ready."

Prue obediently tugged away at the crane, with its black hooks, from which hung the iron tea-kettle and three-legged pot; then she settled the long spit in the grooves made for it in the tall andirons, and put the dripping-pan underneath, for in those days meat was roasted as it should be, not baked in ovens.

Meantime Tilly attacked the plum-pudding. She felt pretty sure of coming out right, here, for she had seen her mother do it so many times, it looked very easy. So in went suet and fruit; all sorts of spice, to be sure she got the right ones, and brandy instead of wine. But she forgot both sugar and salt, and tied it in the cloth so tightly that it had no room to swell, so it would come out as heavy as lead and as hard as a cannon-ball, if the bag did not burst and spoil it all. Happily unconscious of these mistakes, Tilly popped it into the pot, and proudly watched it bobbing about before she put the cover on and left it to its fate.

"I can't remember what flavorin' Ma puts in," she said, when she had got her bread well soaked for the stuffing. "Sage and onions and applesauce go with goose, but I can't feel sure of anything but pepper and salt for a turkey."

"Ma puts in some kind of mint, I know, but I forget whether it is spearmint, peppermint, or pennyroyal," answered Prue, in a tone of doubt, but trying to show her knowledge of "yarbs," or, at least, of their names.

"Seems to me it's sweet marjoram or summer savory. I guess we'll put both in, and then we are sure to be right. The best is up garret; you run and get some, while I mash the bread," commanded Tilly, diving into the mess.

Away trotted Prue, but in her haste she got cat-nip and wormwood, for the garret was darkish, and Prue's little nose was so full of the smell of the onions she had been peeling, that everything smelt of them. Eager to be of use, she pounded up the herbs and scattered the mixture with a liberal hand into the bowl.

"It doesn't smell just right, but I suppose it will when it is cooked," said Tilly, as she filled the empty stomach, that seemed aching for food, and sewed it up with the blue yarn, which happened to be handy. She forgot to tie down his legs and wings, but she set him by till his hour came, well satisfied with her work.

"Shall we roast the little pig, too? I think he'd look nice with a necklace of sausages, as Ma fixed him at Christmas," asked Prue, elated with their success.

"I couldn't do it. I loved that little pig, and cried when he was killed. I should feel as if I was roasting the baby," answered Tilly, glancing toward the buttery where piggy hung, looking so pink and pretty it certainly did seem cruel to eat him.

It took a long time to get all the vegetables ready, for, as the cellar was full, the girls thought they would have every sort. Eph helped, and by noon all was ready for cooking, and the cranberry-sauce, a good deal scorched, was cooking in the lean-to.

Luncheon was a lively meal, and doughnuts and cheese vanished in such quantities that Tilly feared no one would have an appetite for her sumptuous dinner. The boys assured her they would be starving by five o'clock, and Sol mourned bitterly over the little pig that was not to be served up.

"Now you all go and coast, while Prue and I set the table and get out the best chiny," said Tilly, bent on having her dinner look well, no matter what its other failings might be.

Out came the rough sleds, on went the round hoods, old hats, red cloaks, and moccasins, and away

trudged the four younger Bassetts, to disport themselves in the snow, and try the ice down by the old
mill, where the great wheel turned and splashed so
merrily in the summer-time.

Eph took his fiddle and scraped away to his
heart's content in the parlor, while the girls, after a
short rest, set the table and made all ready to dish
up the dinner when that exciting moment came. It
was not at all the sort of table we see now, but
would look very plain and countrified to us, with
its green-handled knives, and two-pronged steel
forks; its red-and-white china, and pewter platters,
scoured till they shone, with mugs and spoons to
match, and a brown jug for the cider. The cloth was
coarse, but white as snow, and the little maids had
seen the blue-eyed flax grow, out of which their
mother wove the linen; they had watched and
watched while it bleached in the green meadow.
They had no napkins and little silver; but the best
tankard and Ma's few wedding-spoons were set
forth in state. Nuts and apples at the corners gave
an air, and the place of honor was left in the middle for the oranges yet to come.

"Don't it look beautiful?" said Prue, when they
paused to admire the general effect.

"Pretty nice, I think. I wish Ma could see how
well we can do it," began Tilly, when a loud howling startled both girls, and sent them flying to the
window. The short afternoon had passed so quickly

that twilight had come before they knew it, and now, as they looked out through the gathering dusk, they saw four small black figures tearing up the road, to come bursting in, all screaming at once: "The bear, the bear! Eph, get the gun! He's coming, he's coming!"

Eph had dropped his fiddle, and got down his gun before the girls could calm the children enough to tell their story, which they did in a somewhat incoherent manner. "Down in the holler, coastin', we heard a growl," began Sol, with his eyes as big as saucers. "I see him fust lookin' over the wall," roared Seth, eager to get his share of honor.

"Awful big and shaggy," quavered Roxy, clinging to Tilly, while Rhody hid in Prue's skirts, and piped out: "His great paws kept clawing at us, and I was so scared my legs would hardly go."

"We ran away as fast as we could go, and he came growlin' after us. He's awful hungry, and he'll eat every one of us if he gets in," continued Sol, looking about him for a safe retreat.

"Oh, Eph, don't let him eat us," cried both little girls, flying upstairs to hide under their mother's bed, as their surest shelter.

"No danger of that, you little geese. I'll shoot him as soon as he comes. Get out of the way, boys," and Eph raised the window to get good aim.

"There he is! Fire away, and don't miss!" cried Seth, hastily following Sol, who had climbed to the top of the dresser as a good perch from which to view the approaching fray.

Prue retired to the hearth as if bent on dying at her post rather than desert the turkey, now "browning beautiful," as she expressed it. But Tilly boldly stood at the open window, ready to lend a hand if the enemy proved too much for Eph.

All had seen bears, but none had ever come so near before, and even brave Eph felt that the big brown beast slowly trotting up the door-yard was an unusually formidable specimen. He was growling horribly, and stopped now and then as if to rest and shake himself.

"Get the ax, Tilly, and if I should miss, stand ready to keep him off while I load again," said Eph, anxious to kill his first bear in style and alone; a girl's help didn't count.

Tilly flew for the ax, and was at her brother's side by the time the bear was near enough to be dangerous. He stood on his hind legs, and seemed to sniff with relish the savory odors that poured out of the window.

"Fire, Eph!" cried Tilly, firmly.

"Wait till he rears again. I'll get a better shot then," answered the boy, while Prue covered her ears to shut out the bang, and the small boys cheered from their dusty refuge up among the pumpkins.

But a very singular thing happened next, and all who saw it stood amazed, for suddenly Tilly threw down the ax, flung open the door, and ran straight into the arms of the bear, who stood erect to receive her, while his growlings changed to a loud "Haw, haw!" that startled the children more than the report of a gun.

"It's Gad Hopkins, tryin' to fool us!" cried Eph, much disgusted at the loss of his prey, for these hardy boys loved to hunt, and prided themselves on the number of wild animals and birds they could shoot in a year.

"Oh, Gad, how could you scare us so?" laughed Tilly, still held fast in one shaggy arm of the bear, while the other drew a dozen oranges from some deep pocket in the buffalo-skin coat, and fired them into the kitchen with such good aim that Eph ducked, Prue screamed, and Sol and Seth came down much quicker than they went up.

"Wal, you see I got upsot over yonder, and the old horse went home while I was floundering in a drift, so I tied on the buffalers to tote 'em easy, and come along till I see the children playin' in the holler. I jest meant to give 'em a little scare, but they run like partridges, and I kep' up the joke to see how Eph would like this sort of company," and Gad haw-hawed again.

"You'd have had a warm welcome if we hadn't found you out. I'd have put a bullet through you in a jiffy, old chap," said Eph, coming out to shake hands with the young giant, who was only a year or two older than himself.

"Come in and set up to dinner with us. Prue and I have done it all ourselves, and Pa will be along soon, I reckon," cried Tilly, trying to escape.

"Couldn't, no ways. My folks will think I'm dead ef I don't get along home, sence the horse and sleigh have gone ahead empty. I've done my arrant and had my joke; now I want my pay, Tilly," and Gad took a hearty kiss from the rosy cheeks of his "little sweetheart," as he called her. His own cheeks tingled with the smart slap she gave him as she ran away, calling out that she hated bears and would bring her ax next time.

"I ain't afeared—your sharp eyes found me out; and ef you run into a bear's arms you must expect a hug," answered Gad, as he pushed back the robe and settled his fur cap more becomingly.

"I should have known you in a minute if I hadn't been asleep when the girls squalled. You did it well, though, and I advise you not to try it again in a hurry, or you'll get shot," said Eph, as they parted, he rather crestfallen and Gad in high glee.

"My sakes alive—the turkey is all burnt one side, and the kettles have biled over so the pies I put to warm are all ashes!" scolded Tilly, as the flurry subsided and she remembered her dinner.

"Well, I can't help it. I couldn't think of victuals when I expected to be eaten alive myself, could I?" pleaded poor Prue, who had tumbled into the cradle when the rain of oranges began.

Tilly laughed, and all the rest joined in, so good-humor was restored, and the spirits of the younger ones were revived by sucks from the one orange which passed from hand to hand with great rapidity while the older girls dished up the dinner. They were just struggling to get the pudding out of the cloth when Roxy called out: "Here's Pa!"

"There's folks with him," added Rhody.

"Lots of 'em! I see two big sleighs chock full," shouted Seth, peering through the dusk.

"It looks like a semintary. Guess Gran'ma's dead and come up to be buried here," said Sol, in a solemn tone. This startling suggestion made Tilly, Prue, and Eph hasten to look out, full of dismay at such an ending of their festival.

"If that is a funeral, the mourners are uncommonly jolly," said Eph, dryly, as merry voices and loud laughter broke the white silence without.

"I see Aunt Cinthy, and Cousin Hetty—and there's Mose and Amos. I do declare, Pa's bringin' 'em all home to have some fun here," cried Prue, as she recognized one familiar face after another.

"Oh, my patience! Ain't I glad I got dinner, and don't I hope it will turn out good!" exclaimed Tilly, while the twins pranced with delight, and the small boys roared:

"Hooray for Pa! Hooray for Thanksgivin'!"

The cheer was answered heartily, and in came Father, Mother, Baby, aunts, and cousins, all in great spirits, and all much surprised to find such a festive welcome awaiting them.

"Ain't Gran'ma dead at all?" asked Sol, in the midst of the kissing and hand-shaking.

"Bless your heart, no! It was all a mistake of old Mr. Chadwick's. He's as deaf as an adder, and when Mrs. Brooks told him Mother was mendin' fast, and she wanted me to come down to-day, certain sure, he got the message all wrong, and give it to the fust person passin' in such a way as to scare me 'most to death, and send us down in a hurry. Mother was sittin' up as chirk as you please, and dreadful sorry you didn't all come."

"So, to keep the house quiet for her, and give you a taste of the fun, your Pa fetched us all up to spend the evenin', and we are goin' to have a jolly time on't, to jedge by the looks of things," said Aunt Cinthy, briskly finishing the tale when Mrs. Bassett paused for want of breath.

"What in the world put it into your head we was comin', and set you to gittin' up such a supper?" asked Mr. Bassett, looking about him, well pleased and much surprised at the plentiful table.

Tilly modestly began to tell, but the others broke in and sang her praises in a sort of chorus, in which bears, pigs, pies, and oranges were oddly mixed. Great satisfaction was expressed by all, and Tilly and Prue were so elated by the commendation of Ma and the aunts, that they set forth their dinner, sure everything was perfect.

But when the eating began, which it did the moment wraps were off, then their pride got a fall; for the first person who tasted the stuffing (it was big Cousin Mose, and that made it harder to bear) nearly choked over the bitter morsel.

"Tilly Bassett, whatever made you put worm-wood and catnip in your stuffin'?" demanded Ma, trying not to be severe, for all the rest were laughing, and Tilly looked ready to cry.

"I did it," said Prue, nobly taking all the blame, which caused Pa to kiss her on the spot, and declare that it didn't do a mite of harm, for the turkey was all right.

"I never see onions cooked better. All the vegetables is well done, and the dinner a credit to you, my dears," declared Aunt Cinthy, with her mouth full of the fragrant vegetable she praised.

The pudding was an utter failure in spite of the blazing brandy in which it lay—as hard and heavy as one of the stone balls on Squire Dunkin's great gate. It was speedily whisked out of sight, and all fell upon the pies, which were perfect. But Tilly and Prue were much depressed, and didn't recover their spirits till dinner was over and the evening fun well under way.

"Blind-man's bluff," "Hunt the slipper," "Come, Philander," and other lively games soon set every one bubbling over with jollity, and when Eph struck up "Money Musk" on his fiddle, old and young fell into their places for a dance. All down the long kitchen they stood, Mr. and Mrs. Bassett at the top, the twins at the bottom, and then away they went, heeling and toeing, cutting pigeon-wings, and taking their steps in a way that would convulse modern children with their new-fangled romps called dancing. Mose and Tilly covered themselves with glory by the vigor with which they kept it up, till fat Aunt Cinthy fell into a chair, breathlessly declaring that a very little of such exercise was enough for a woman of her "heft."

Apples and cider, chat and singing, finished the evening, and after a grand kissing all round, the guests drove away in the clear moonlight which came out to cheer their long drive.

When the jingle of the last bell had died away, Mr. Bassett said soberly, as they stood together on the hearth: "Children, we have special cause to be thankful that the sorrow we expected was changed into joy, so we'll read a chapter 'fore we go to bed, and give thanks where thanks is due."

Then Tilly set out the light-stand with the big Bible on it, and a candle on each side, and all sat quietly in the fire-light, smiling as they listened with happy hearts to the sweet old words that fit all times and seasons so beautifully.

When the good-nights were over, and the children in bed, Prue put her arm round Tilly and whispered tenderly, for she felt her shake, and was sure she was crying:

"Don't mind about the old stuffin' and puddin', deary—nobody cared, and Ma said we really did do surprisin' well for such young girls."

The laughter Tilly was trying to smother broke out then, and was so infectious, Prue could not help joining her, even before she knew the cause of the merriment.

"I was mad about the mistakes, but don't care enough to cry. I'm laughing to think how Gad fooled Eph and I found him out. I thought Mose and Amos would have died over it, when I told them, it was so funny," explained Tilly, when she got her breath.

"I was so scared that when the first orange hit me, I thought it was a bullet, and scrabbled into the cradle as fast as I could.

It was real mean to frighten the little ones so," laughed Prue, as Tilly gave a growl.

Here a smart rap on the wall of the next room caused a sudden lull in the fun, and Mrs. Bassett's voice was heard, saying warningly, "Girls, go to sleep immediate, or you'll wake the baby."

"Yes'm," answered two meek voices, and after a few irrepressible giggles, silence reigned, broken only by an occasional snore from the boys, or the soft scurry of mice in the buttery, taking their part in this old-fashioned Thanksgiving.

Christmas Waits in Boston

[EDWARD EVERETT HALE]

I

I always give myself a Christmas present. And on this particular year the present was a Carol party,—which is about as good fun, all things consenting kindly, as a man can have.

Many things must consent, as will appear. First of all there must be good sleighing,—and second, a fine night for Chrismas Eve. Ours are not the carollings of your poor shivering little East Angles or South Mercians, where they have to plod around afoot in countries where they do not know what a sleigh-ride is.

I had asked Harry to have sixteen of the best voices in the chapel school to be trained to eight or ten good carols without knowing why. We did not

care to disappoint them if a February thaw setting in on the twenty-fourth of December should
break up the spree before it began. Then I had
told Howland that he must reserve for me a span
of good horses and a sleigh that I could pack sixteen small children into, tight-stowed. Howland
is always good about such things, knew what the
sleigh was for, having done the same in other years,
and doubled the span of horses of his own accord,
because the children would like it better, and "it
would be no difference to him." Sunday night, as
the weather nymphs ordered, the wind hauled
round to the northwest and everything froze hard.
Monday night things moderated, and the snow
began to fall steadily,—so steadily;—and so Tuesday night the Metropolitan people gave up their
unequal contest, all good men and angels rejoicing
at their discomfiture, and only a few of the people
in the very lowest *Bolgie* being ill-natured enough
to grieve. And thus it was, that by Thursday
evening there was one hard compact roadway from
Copp's Hill to the Bone-burner's Gehenna, fit for
good men and angels to ride over, without jar,
without noise, and without fatigue to horse or
man. So it was that when I came down with Lycidas to the chapel at seven o'clock, I found Harry
had gathered there his eight pretty girls and his
eight jolly boys, and had them practising for the
last time:

"Carol, carol Christians,
Carol joyfully;
Carol for the coming
Of Christ's nativity."

I think the children had got inkling of what was coming, or perhaps Harry had hinted it to their mothers. Certainly they were warmly dressed, and when, fifteen minutes afterwards, Howland came round himself with the sleigh, he had put in as many rugs and bear-skins as if he thought the children were to be taken new-born from their respective cradles. Great was the rejoicing as the bells of the horses rang beneath the chapel windows, and Harry did not get his last *da capo* for his last carol, not much matter indeed, for they were perfect enough in it before midnight.

Lycidas and I tumbled in on the back seat, each with a child on his lap to keep us warm; I was flanked by Sam Perry, and he by John Rich, both of the mercurial age, and therefore good to do errands. Harry was in front somewhere, flanked in likewise, and the twelve other children lay in miscellaneously between, like sardines when you have first opened the box. I had invited Lycidas, because, besides being my best friend, he is the best fellow in the world, and so deserves the best Christmas Eve can give him. Under the full moon, on the snow still white, with sixteen children at the happiest, and with the blessed memories of the best the world has ever had, there can be nothing better than two or three such hours.

"First, driver, out on Commonwealth Avenue. That will tone down the horses. Stop on the left after you have passed Fairfield Street." So we dashed up to the front of Haliburton's palace, where he was keeping his first Christmastide. And the children, whom Harry had hushed down for a square or two, broke forth with good full voice under his strong lead in

"Shepherd of tender sheep,"

singing with all that unconscious pathos with which children do sing, and starting the tears in your eyes in the midst of your gladness. The instant the horses' bells stopped, their voices began. In an instant more we saw Haliburton and Anna run to the window and pull up the shades, and, in a minute more, faces at all the windows. And so the children sung through Clement's old hymn. Little did Clement think of bells and snow, as he taught it in his Sunday school there in Alexandria. But perhaps to-day, as they pin up the laurels and the palm in the chapel at Alexandria, they are humming the words, not thinking of Clement more than he thought of us. As the children closed with

"Swell the triumphant song
    To Christ, our King,"

Haliburton came running out, and begged me to bring them in. But I told him, "No," as soon as I could hush their shouts of "Merry Christmas;" that we had a long journey before us, and must not alight by the way. And the children broke out with

> "Hail to the night,
> Hail to the day,"

rather a favorite,—quicker and more to the childish taste, perhaps, than the other,—and with another "Merry Christmas" we were off again.

Off, the length of Commonwealth Avenue, to where it crosses the Brookline branch of the Mill-Dam,—dashing along with the gayest of sleighing-parties as we came back into town, up Chestnut Street, through Louisburg Square,—we ran the sleigh into a bank on the slope of Pinckney Street in front of Walter's house,—and before they suspected there that any one had come, the children were singing

> "Carol, carol Christians,
> Carol joyfully."

Kisses flung from the window; kisses flung back from the street. "Merry Christmas" again and a good-will, and then one of the girls began

"When Anna took the baby,
  And pressed his lips to hers"—

and all of them fell in so cheerily. O dear me! it is
a scrap of old Ephrem the Syrian, if they did but
know it! And when, after this Harry, would fain
have driven on, how the little witches begged that
they might sing just one song more there, because
Mrs. Alexander had been so kind to them, when
she showed them about the German stitches. And
then up the hill and over to the North End, and as
far as we could get the horses up into Moon
Court, that they might sing to the Italian image-
man who gave Lucy the boy and dog in plaster,
when she was sick in the spring. For the children
had, you know, the choice of where they would
go; and they select their best friends, and will be
more apt to remember the Italian image-man than
Chrysostom himself, though Chrysostom should
have "made a few remarks" to them seventeen
times in the chapel. Then the Italian image-man
heard for the first time in his life:

"Now is the time of Christmas come,"

and

"Jesus in his babes abiding."

And then we came up Hanover Street and stopped under Mr. Gerry's chapel, where they were dressing the walls with their evergreens, and gave them

"Hail to the night,
  Hail to the day."

And so down State Street and stopped at the *Advertiser* office, because when the boys gave their Literary Entertainment, Mr. Hale put in their advertisement for nothing, and up in the old attic there the compositors were relieved to hear

"No war nor battle sound,"

and

"The waiting world was still."

Even the leading editor relaxed from his gravity and the "In General" man from his more serious views, and the *Daily* the next morning wished everybody a "Merry Christmas" with even more unction, and resolved that in coming years it would have a supplement, large enough to contain all the good wishes. So away again to the houses of confectioners who had given the children candy,—to Miss Simonds' house, because she had been so good to them in school,—to the palaces of millionaires who had prayed for these children with tears if the children only knew it,—to Dr. Frothingham in Summer Street, I remember, where we stopped because the Boston Association of Ministers met there,—and out on Dover Street Bridge, that the poor chair mender might hear our carols sung once more before he heard them better sung in another world where nothing needs mending. . . . O, we went to twenty places that night, I suppose; we went to the grandest places in Boston, and we went to the meanest. At nine we brought up at my house, D Street, three doors from the corner, and the children picked out their very best for Polly and my six little girls to hear, and then for the first time we let them jump out and run in. Polly had some hot oysters for them, so that the frolic was crowned with a treat. There was a Christmas cake cut into sixteen pieces, which they took home to dream upon; and then hoods and mufflers on again, and by ten o'clock or a little after, we had all the girls and all the little ones at their homes . . .

Lycidas and I both thought that the welcome of these homes was perhaps the best part of it all, as we went into these modest houses, to leave the children, to say they had been good, and to wish a "Merry Christmas" ourselves to fathers, mothers, and to guardian aunts. . . . Here was brave Mrs.

Masury. I had not seen her since her mother died.
"Indeed, Mr. Ingham, I got so used to watching
then, that I cannot sleep well yet o'nights; I wish
you knew some poor creature that wanted me to-
night, if it were only in memory of Bethlehem" . . .
"What can I send to your children," said Dalton,
who was finishing sword-blades. (Ill wind was Fort
Sumter, but it blew good to poor Dalton, whom it
set up in the world with his sword-factory.) "Here's
an old-fashioned tape-measure for the girl, and a
Sheffield wimble for the boy. What, there is no
boy? Let one of the girls have it, then; it will count
one more present for her." And so he pressed his
brown-paper parcel into my hand. From every
house, though it were the humblest, a word of love,
as sweet, in truth, as if we could have heard the voice
of angels singing in the sky.

I bade Harry good-night; took Lycidas to his
house, and gave his wife my Christmas wishes and
good-night; and, coming down to the sleigh again,
gave way to the feeling which I think you will all
understand, that this was not the time to stop, but
just the time to begin. For the streets were stilled
now, and the moon brighter than ever, and the
blessings of these simple people and of the proud
people, and of the very angels in heaven, who are
not bound to the misery of using words when they
have anything worth saying,—all these wishes and
blessings were round me, all the purity of the still

winter night, and I didn't want to lose it all by
going to bed to sleep. So I put the boys all together,
where they could chatter, and then, pasting through
Charles Street . . . I noticed the lights in Woodhull's
house, and, seeing they were up, thought I would
make Fanny a midnight call. She came to the door
herself. I asked if she were waiting for Santa Claus,
but I saw in a moment that I must not joke with
her. She said she had hoped I was her husband. In a
minute was one of those contrasts which make life,
life . . . Poor Fanny's mother had been blocked up in
the Springfield train as she was coming on for
Christmas. The old lady had been chilled through,
and was here in bed now with pneumonia. Both
Fanny's children had been ailing when she came, and
this morning the doctor had pronounced it scarlet
fever. Fanny had not undressed herself since Monday, nor slept, I thought, in the same time. So while
we had been singing carols and wishing Merry
Christmas, the poor child had been waiting, hoping
that her husband or Edward, both of whom were
on the tramp, would find for her and bring to her
the model nurse, who had not yet arrived, nor had
either of the men returned. Professional paragons,
dear reader, are shy of scarlet fever. I told the poor
child that it was better as it was. I wrote a line for
Sam Perry to take to his aunt, Mrs. Masury, in
which I simply said: "Dear mamma, I have found
the poor creature who wants you to-night. Come

back in this carriage." I bade him take a hack at Barnard's, where they were all up waiting for the assembly to be done at Papanti's. I sent him over to Albany Street; and really as I sat there trying to soothe Fanny, it seemed to me less time than it has taken me to dictate this little story about her, before Mrs. Masury rang gently, and I left them, having made Fanny promise that she would consecrate the day, which at that moment was born, by trusting God, by going to bed and going to sleep, knowing that her children were in much better hands than hers . . .

And so I walked home. Better so, perhaps, after all, than in the lively sleigh with the tinkling bells. What an eternity it seemed since I started with those children singing carols!

> "Within that province far away
>
>   Went plodding home a weary boor;
>
>   A streak of light before him lay,
>
>   Fallen through a half-shut stable door
>
>   Across his path. He passed, for naught
>
>   Told what was going on within:
>
>   How keen the stars, his only thought,
>
>   The air how calm and cold and thin,
>
>   In the solemn midnight,
>
>   Centuries ago!"

"Streak of light"—Is there a light in Lycidas's room? They not in bed? That is making a night of

it! Well, there are few hours of the day or night
when I have not been in Lycidas's room, so I let
myself in by the night-key he gave me, and ran up
the stairs,—it is a horrid seven-storied first-class,
apartment-house. For my part, I had as lief live in
a steeple. Two flights I ran up, two steps at a time,—
I was younger then than I am now,—pushed open
the door which was ajar, and saw such a scene of
confusion as I never saw in Mary's over-nice parlor
before. Queer! I remember the first thing that I saw
was wrong was a great ball of white German worsted
on the floor. Her basket was upset. A great Christmas tree lay across the rug, quite too high for the
room; a large, sharp-pointed Spanish clasp-knife
was by it, with which they had been lopping it;
there were two immense baskets of white papered
presents, both upset; but what frightened me most
was the centre-table. Three or four handkerchiefs
on it,—towels, napkins, I know not what,—all
brown and red and almost black with blood! I
turned, heart-sick, to look into the bedroom,—and
I really had a sense of relief when I saw somebody . . . Lycidas, but just now so strong and well,
lay pale and exhausted . . . while over him bent
Mary and Morton. I learned afterwards that poor
Lycidas, while trimming the Christmas tree and
talking merrily with Mary and Morton,—who, by
good luck, had brought round his presents late, and
was staying to tie on glass balls and apples,—had

given himself a deep and dangerous wound with the point of the unlucky knife, and had lost a great deal of blood before the hemorrhage could be controlled. Just before I entered, the stick tourniquet which Morton had temporised had slipped in poor Mary's unpractised hand, at the moment he was about to secure the artery . . .

"O Fred," said Morton, without looking up, "I am glad you are here."

"And what can I do for you?"

"Some whiskey,—first of all."

"There are two bottles," said Mary, "in the cupboard behind his dressing-glass."

I took Bridget with me, struck a light in the dressing-room (how she blundered about the match) and found the cupboard door locked! Key doubtless in Mary's pocket,—probably in pocket of "another dress." I did not ask. Took my own bunch, willed tremendously that my account-book drawer key should govern the lock, and it did. If it had not, I should have put my fist through the panels. Bottle marked "bay rum;" another bottle with no mark; two bottles of Saratoga water. "Set them all on the floor, Bridget." A tall bottle of cologne. Bottle marked in manuscript. What in the world is it? "Bring that candle, Bridget." "Eau distillée, Marron, Montreal." What in the world did Lycidas bring distilled water from Montreal for? And then Morton's clear voice from the other room, "As quick as you can, Fred." "Yes! in one moment. Put all these on the floor, Bridget." Here they are at last. "Corkscrew, Bridget."

"Indade, sir, and where is it?" "Where? I don't know. Run as quick as you can, and bring it. His wife cannot leave him." So Bridget ran, and I meanwhile am driving a silver pronged fork into the Bourbon corks, and the blade of my own penknife for the other side.

"Now, Fred," from Morton, within. "Yes, in one moment," I replied. Penknife blade breaks off, fork pulls right out, two crumbs of cork with it. Will that girl never come?

I turned round; I found a goblet on the washstand; I took Lycidas's heavy clothes-brush and knocked off the neck of the bottle . . . It smashed like a Prince Rupert's drop in my hand, crumbled into seventy pieces,—a nasty smell of whiskey on the floor,—and I, holding just the hard bottom of the thing with two large spikes running worthless up into the air. But I seized the goblet, poured into it what was left in the bottom, and carried it into Morton as quietly as I could. He bade me give Lycidas as much as he could swallow; then showed me how to compress the great artery. When he was satisfied that he could trust me, he began his work again, silently. . . . When all was secure, he glanced at the ghastly white face, with beads of perspiration on the forehead and upper lip, laid his finger on the pulse and said, "We will have a little more whiskey. No, Mary, you are overdone already; let Fred bring it." The truth was that poor Mary was almost as white as Lycidas. She would not faint,— that was the only reason she did not,—and at the moment I wondered that she did not fall. Bridget, you see, was still nowhere. So I retired again, to attack that other bottle. Would that Kelt ever come? I passed the bell-rope as I went into the dressing-room, and rang as hard as I could ring. I took the other bottle and bit steadily with my teeth at the cork, only, of course, to wrench the end of it off. Morton called me, and I stepped back. "No," said he, "bring your whiskey."

Mary had just rolled gently back on the floor. I went again in despair. But I heard Bridget's step this time. She ran in, in triumph, with a *screw-driver!*

"No!" I whispered,—"no. The crooked thing you draw corks with," and I showed her the bottle again. "Find one somewhere and don't come back without it."

"Frederic!" said Morton. I think he never called me so before . . . "Frederic!" "Yes," I said. But why did I say "Yes"? "Father of Mercy, tell me what to do."

And my mazed eyes, dim with tears,—did you ever shed tears from excitement?—fell on an old razor-strop of those days of shaving, made by *C. Whittaker,* SHEFFIELD. The Sheffield stood in black letters out from the rest like a vision. They make corkscrews in Sheffield too. If this Whittaker had only made a corkscrew! And what is a "Sheffield wimble?"

Hand in my pocket—brown paper parcel.

"Where are you, Frederic?" "Yes," said I for the last time. Twine off! brown paper off! And I learned that the "Sheffield wimble" was one of those things whose name you never heard before, which people sell you in Thames Tunnel, where a hoof-cleaner, a gimlet, a screw-driver and a *corkscrew* fold into one handle. "Yes," said I again. "Pop," said the cork. "Bubble, bubble, bubble," said the whiskey. Bottle in one hand, full tumbler in the other, I walked in. Morton poured half a tumblerful down Lycidas's throat that time . . . I found that there was need of it, from what he said of the pulse when it was all over . . .

This was the turning-point. He was exceedingly weak, and we sat by him through the night, . . . but there was no real danger after that.

As we turned away from the house on Christmas morning,—I to preach and he to visit his patients,— he said to me, "Did you *make* that whiskey?"

"No," said I, "but poor Dod Dalton had to furnish the corkscrew."

And I went down to the chapel to preach. The sermon had been lying ready at home on my desk, and Polly had brought it round to me, for there had been no time for me to go from Lycidas's home to

D Street and to return. There was the text, all as it was the day before:

> They helped every one his neighbor, and every one said to his brother, Be of good courage. So the carpenter encouraged the goldsmith, and he that smootheth with the hammer him that smote the anvil.

And there were the pat illustrations, as I had finished them yesterday . . . And I said to them all, "O, if I could tell you, my friends, what every twelve hours of my life tells me,—of the way in which woman helps woman, and man helps man, when only the ice is broken,—how we are all rich as soon as we find out that we are all brothers, and how we are all in want, unless we can call at any moment for a brother's hand,—then I could make you understand something, in the lives you lead every day, of what the New Covenant, the New Commonwealth, the New Kingdom, is to be . . ."

But when we had our tree in the evening at home, I did tell all this story to Polly and the bairns, and I gave Alice her measuring tape,—precious with a spot of Lycidas's blood,—and Bertha her Sheffield wimble. "Papa," said old Clara, who is the next child, "all the people gave presents, did not they, as they did in the picture in your study?"

"Yes," said I, "though they did not all know they were giving them."

"Why do they not give such presents every day?" said Clara.

"O child," I said, "it is only for thirty-six hours of the three hundred and sixty-five days that all people remember that they are all brothers and sisters, and those are the hours that we call, therefore, Christmas Eve and Christmas Day."

Sources

"Old Deb and Other Old Colony Witches," from *The Old Colony Town and Other Sketches*, William Root Bliss, 1893.

"The Wraith in the Storm," from *The Myths and Fables of To-Day*, Samuel Adams Drake, 1900.

"Jonathan Moulton and the Devil," from *A Book of New England Legends and Folk Lore*, Samuel Adams Drake, 1883.

"The Spouter-Inn," "The Counterpane," "Breakfast," "The Street," "The Chapel," and "Nantucket," from *Moby-Dick*, Herman Melville, 1851.

"Marsh Rosemary," from *Tales of New England*, Sarah Orne Jewett, 1890.

"Young Goodman Brown," from *Mosses from an Old Manse*, Nathaniel Hawthorne, 1846.

"Miss Mehetabel's Son," from *Marjorie Daw and Other People*, Thomas Bailey Aldrich, 1873.

"Fire-Worship," from *Mosses from an Old Manse*, Nathaniel Hawthorne, 1846.

"Law Lane," from *Tales of New England*, Sarah Orne Jewett, 1890.

"Turkeys and a Footrace," from *Farming It*, Henry A. Shute, 1909.

"The Calf—Another Footrace," from *Farming It*, Henry A. Shute, 1909.

"An Old-Fashioned Thanksgiving," from *St. Nicholas* magazine, Louisa May Alcott, 1881.

"Christmas Waits in Boston," from *Christmas Eve and Christmas Day*, Edward Everett Hale, 1894.